EMPOWER, ENGAGE, EDUCATE

(TOOLKIT FOR CLASSROOM MANAGEMENT)

DR. MAN MOHAN SINGH

INDIA • SINGAPORE • MALAYSIA

ISBN
Paperback 979-8-89632-384-6
Hardcase 979-8-89673-496-3

Contents

Ten Commandments

1. **Inspire a Love of Learning**: Foster curiosity and a passion for knowledge in your students.
2. **Be a Role Model**: Demonstrate integrity, respect, and a strong work ethic in all that you do.
3. **Encourage Critical Thinking**: Challenge students to ask questions, think deeply, and engage in problem-solving.
4. **Cultivate a Safe Environment**: Create a classroom atmosphere where every student feels valued and secure.
5. **Adapt and Innovate**: Be flexible in your teaching methods and open to new ideas and technologies.
6. **Communicate Clearly**: Ensure that your instructions and feedback are clear and constructive.
7. **Show Empathy and Understanding**: Recognize the individual needs and challenges of each student.
8. **Promote Collaboration**: Encourage teamwork and respect for diverse perspectives among students.
9. **Continue Learning**: Pursue professional development and stay informed about best practices in education.
10. **Celebrate Achievements**: Acknowledge and celebrate the successes of your students, no matter how small.

(These principles can help create a positive and effective learning environment)

Foreword

"Empower, Engage, Educate"

Empower

- **Leadership Skills**: Provide educators with tools to lead within their classrooms and schools, encouraging them to take initiative and drive change.
- **Confidence Building**: Workshops and coaching sessions that focus on self-efficacy and resilience can help teachers feel more capable and confident in their roles.
- **Resource Accessibility**: Ensure that teachers have access to up-to-date resources, technology, and support systems that enable them to thrive.

Engage

- **Interactive Learning**: Use collaborative workshops, peer mentoring, and hands-on activities to create a dynamic learning atmosphere.
- **Real-World Application**: Encourage teachers to bring their own experiences into the training, making learning relevant and practical.
- **Feedback Loops**: Establish systems for ongoing feedback from educators to tailor professional development to their needs and interests.

Educate

- **Continuous Learning**: Offer regular training sessions on the latest educational research, teaching strategies, and technologies.
- **Diverse Perspectives**: Include a variety of educational philosophies and methodologies to broaden teachers' approaches.
- **Assessment and Reflection**: Provide tools for educators to assess their own teaching practices and reflect on their professional growth.

Implementation Strategies

- **Coaching and Mentorship**: Pair less experienced educators with mentors to foster growth and collaboration.
- **Professional Learning Communities (PLCs)**: Create spaces for educators to share insights, challenges, and strategies.
- **Flexible Learning Options**: Offer online courses, workshops, and seminars to accommodate different schedules and learning preferences.

This approach not only enhances individual teaching practices but also contributes to a more engaged and effective learning environment for students.

In an ever-evolving educational landscape, teachers are the backbone of our learning communities, guiding and inspiring students to reach their fullest potential. This toolkit is designed as a beacon of support for educators, offering practical strategies, resources, and insights that can transform the classroom experience.

As teachers, we are constantly faced with new challenges, from diverse student needs to integrating technology effectively. This book serves not only as a guide but as a companion on your journey—equipping you with the tools to foster engagement, differentiate instruction, and create an inclusive environment where every student can thrive.

Whether you are a seasoned educator or just starting your teaching career, the resources within these pages are intended to spark creativity, inspire collaboration, and empower you to make a lasting impact. Let this toolkit be a source of inspiration and a reminder that you are not alone in this vital work.

Teaching is more than just a profession; it is a profound calling. Every day, you step into the classroom, ready to inspire, nurture, and guide the next generation. Your dedication shapes not only academic success but also the character and future of your students.

In this ever-changing world, your role is more important than ever. You are not just imparting knowledge; you are fostering critical thinkers, encouraging creativity, and instilling values that will last a lifetime. Each lesson you teach and every interaction you have leaves a lasting impact on your students.

This book is designed with you in mind—packed with practical strategies, innovative ideas, and insights to support you in your journey. Remember, it's okay to seek help, share your challenges, and celebrate your victories. You are part of a vibrant community of educators who share your passion and commitment.

As you explore the pages ahead, may you find inspiration and encouragement. Your work is vital, and the influence you wield is immeasurable. Thank you for your unwavering commitment to shaping brighter futures.

Together, let's embrace the challenges and joys of teaching, cultivating a brighter future for our students and communities.

Chapter 1

Classroom Management

> ***"For the mind does not require filling like a bottle, but rather, like wood, it only requires kindling to create in it an impulse to think independently and an ardent desire for the truth."***
>
> *— Plutarch*

Classroom management is an art and a science. It is the delicate balance between establishing order and nurturing an environment where creativity, collaboration, and learning can thrive. As educators, we are tasked not only with imparting knowledge but also with shaping the culture of our classrooms—an environment that fosters respect, engagement, and growth.

This book aims to be a guide for both novice and seasoned educators, offering insights and practical strategies to create a learning space that is conducive to both academic success and personal development. It recognizes that no two classrooms are the same, and no single approach to management will work in every situation. Instead, it offers a rich toolbox of approaches—adaptable, flexible, and grounded in research—that can be tailored to meet the unique needs of students.

What stands out in this book is its focus on building positive relationships. It underscores the importance of understanding students' perspectives, connecting with them as individuals, and creating an atmosphere of mutual respect. After all, effective classroom management is not about control or compliance, but about creating a partnership where all participants—the teacher and the students—feel valued and supported.

From setting clear expectations and routines to handling conflicts with empathy and consistency, the strategies presented here will help educators navigate the challenges of the classroom with confidence and compassion. This book serves as both a practical manual and a source of inspiration, reminding us that behind every challenging moment lies an opportunity for growth—for both teacher and student.

In the pages that follow, you will find more than just advice on maintaining order; you will find a blueprint for fostering an environment that celebrates learning, encourages exploration, and builds the foundation for lifelong success. It is my hope that as you read through these pages, you will discover new tools, refine your techniques, and be reminded of the profound impact you can have on the students you teach.

Classroom management is a crucial aspect of effective teaching that involves a series of strategies aimed at creating an o**rganized, efficient, and conducive learning environment**. It encompasses a variety of practices that educators use to **maintain order, promote student engagement, and foster a positive classroom atmosphere**. Effective classroom management not only enhances student learning but also helps **in developing a sense of community within the classroom.**

The Importance of Classroom Management: A well-managed classroom is essential for several reasons. First, **it minimizes disruptions and distractions**, allowing for a more focused learning experience. Students are more likely to **participate actively and engage with the material when they feel safe and respected**. Second, effective management techniques can help in **building strong relationships between teachers and students**, which is vital for fostering trust and open communication. Lastly, a positive classroom environment **encourages student motivation**, which can lead to improved academic performance and behavior.

"Strategies for Effective Classroom Management"

- **Establish Clear Expectations**: One of the first steps in effective classroom management is to set clear rules and expectations. Teachers should **communicate their expectations regarding behavior, participation, and academic integrity from the outset**. Involving students in the creation of these rules can foster a sense of ownership and responsibility.

- **Consistent Routines**: Establishing routines helps students understand what is expected of them throughout the day. Consistent procedures for daily activities—such as entering the classroom, transitioning between tasks, and submitting assignments—can reduce confusion and minimize disruptions.

- **Positive Reinforcement**: Recognizing and rewarding positive behavior can motivate students to adhere to classroom rules. This can be achieved through verbal praise, tangible rewards, or a point system. Positive reinforcement not only acknowledges good behavior but also encourages other students to emulate it.

- **Engagement Techniques**: Keeping students actively engaged in their learning is vital for maintaining order. Incorporating varied instructional strategies—such as group work, hands-on activities, and technology integration—can cater to different learning styles and keep students interested.

- **Proactive Behavior Management**: Anticipating potential disruptions and addressing them before they escalate is a key component of effective classroom management. This can include **rearranging seating, monitoring student interactions, or adjusting lesson pacing to maintain attention**.

- **Building Relationships**: Establishing strong relationships with students can lead to a more **harmonious classroom environment**. Teachers who take the time to understand their students' interests, backgrounds, and needs create a **sense of belonging**, which can reduce behavioral issues.

- **Conflict Resolution**: Conflicts are inevitable in any classroom. Developing strategies for resolving disputes—such as mediation techniques or collaborative problem-solving—can help maintain a respectful environment and teach students valuable life skills.

Classroom management is a multifaceted process that requires **careful planning and execution**. By establishing clear expectations, maintaining consistent routines, employing positive reinforcement, and fostering student engagement, educators can create an environment conducive to learning. Moreover, building **strong relationships** with students and effectively managing conflicts are essential components of a successful classroom. Ultimately, effective classroom management not only **enhances student achievement** but also contributes to the overall well-being of the school community. Through intentional and thoughtful practices, teachers can create a vibrant and supportive learning environment where all students can thrive.

"The Importance of Effective Classroom Management"

> ***"The dream begins, most of the time, with a teacher who believes in you, who tugs and pushes and leads you on to the next plateau, sometimes poking you with a sharp stick called truth."***
>
> *— Dan Rather*

Effective classroom management is a fundamental element of **successful teaching and learning.** It involves the strategies and techniques that educators use to create an organized, respectful, and productive classroom environment. The significance of effective classroom management **extends beyond mere discipline**; it plays a crucial role in enhancing student learning, fostering a positive classroom culture, and promoting overall academic success.

- **Creating a positive learning environment:** At the heart of effective classroom management is the creation of a positive learning environment. When students feel safe, respected, and valued, they are more likely to engage in the learning process. A well-managed classroom minimizes disruptions and distractions, allowing teachers to focus on instruction and students to concentrate on their studies. By establishing clear expectations and routines, educators can foster a sense of stability that supports student engagement and motivation.

- **Enhancing student engagement**: Effective classroom management is directly linked to student engagement. When students understand what is expected of them and feel confident in their learning environment, they are more likely to participate actively in discussions and activities. Engaged students take ownership of their learning, which leads to deeper understanding and retention of material. Techniques such as varied instructional methods, collaborative learning opportunities, and interactive activities can all contribute to heightened engagement, making effective classroom management essential for academic success.

- **Building Strong Teacher-Student Relationships**: Strong relationships between teachers and students are vital for effective classroom management. When students feel connected to their teacher, they are more likely to respect classroom rules and engage in positive behaviors. Building rapport can be achieved through showing interest in students' lives, being approachable and demonstrating empathy. These relationships create a supportive atmosphere where students are more willing to communicate openly, ask for help, and collaborate with peers, further enhancing the learning experience.

- **Reducing Behavioral Issues**: A significant aspect of effective classroom management is the ability to prevent and address behavioral issues. Proactive strategies—such as establishing clear rules, consistent routines, and positive reinforcement—can significantly reduce the occurrence of disruptions. When students understand the consequences of their actions and the benefits of positive behavior, they are more likely to adhere to classroom expectations. Additionally, teachers equipped with conflict resolution skills can manage disputes constructively, maintaining a respectful classroom environment.

- **Promoting Academic Achievement:** Ultimately, effective classroom management is closely tied to academic achievement. When a classroom operates smoothly, students can focus on learning rather than navigating distractions or conflicts. Research shows that classrooms with effective management practices often see higher levels of student achievement and better overall academic performance. By fostering an environment conducive to learning, teachers can help students reach their full potential.

Effective classroom management is essential for **creating a positive, engaging, and productive learning environment**. It not only enhances student engagement and academic achievement but also fosters strong relationships between teachers and students. By implementing proactive strategies and maintaining consistency, educators can minimize behavioral issues and create a supportive atmosphere where all students can thrive.

1. **Communication Skills**: Ability to convey information clearly and engage students.
2. **Patience**: Essential for working with students of varying abilities and learning styles.
3. **Organization**: Skills in planning lessons, managing classroom activities, and track.
4. **Adaptability**: Teaching methods based on student needs & classroom dynamics.
5. **Empathy**: Understanding and addressing the emotional and social needs of students.
6. **Critical Thinking**: Ability to analyze situations, solve problems, and decisions.
7. **Creativity**: Innovating lesson plans and finding engaging ways to present material.
8. **Classroom Management**: Skills in a positive and productive environment.
9. **Collaboration**: Working effectively with colleagues, parents, and community.
10. **Subject knowledge:** A strong understanding of the content being taught.
11. **Assessment Skills**: Ability to evaluate performance & constructive feedback.
12. **Technology Proficiency**: Familiarity with educational technology and tools.

"Overview of How Classroom Management Impacts Learning and Student Behavior"

Classroom management is a critical aspect of effective teaching that significantly influences **both learning outcomes and student behavior.** It encompasses a range of strategies and techniques aimed at creating a structured, respectful, and engaging learning environment. Understanding the dynamics of classroom management provides valuable insights into its profound effects on **student engagement, academic performance, and overall behavior in the classroom.**

The Connection between Classroom Management and Learning: Effective classroom management directly impacts student learning by establishing an environment conducive to education. When teachers implement clear rules, routines, and procedures, students understand what is expected of them, leading to a sense of security and predictability. This stability fosters a focus on learning, as students are less distracted by disruptions and more engaged in instructional activities.

Research indicates that well-managed classrooms **yield higher academic achievement**. Students in such environments are more likely to **participate** actively in lessons, collaborate with peers, and demonstrate greater motivation. When teachers employ varied instructional methods and actively engage students, they not only enhance understanding but also cater to diverse learning styles, further promoting academic success.

The Role of Classroom Management in Shaping Student Behavior: Classroom management plays a pivotal role in influencing student behavior. By setting clear expectations and consistently reinforcing positive behaviors, teachers can create a culture of respect and responsibility. When students know the behavioral standards and the consequences of their actions, they are more likely to comply with classroom norms.

Positive reinforcement strategies, such as **praise and rewards** for good behavior, **encourage students to exhibit desired actions**. Conversely, effective management also involves **addressing disruptive behavior**

promptly and fairly, which helps maintain a respectful learning environment. By managing behavior proactively, teachers can reduce conflicts and minimize disruptions, allowing for a more focused educational experience.

Fostering a positive classroom climate: A well-managed classroom fosters a positive climate where students feel valued and respected. When teachers build strong relationships with their students and promote a sense of community, students are more likely to engage in cooperative behaviors. This positive classroom climate encourages students to take risks in their learning, ask questions, and seek help when needed.

Moreover, a supportive environment can significantly impact **students' social and emotional development**. When students feel safe and accepted, they are more likely to develop self-esteem and resilience, both of which are crucial for long-term success. Effective classroom management thus not only enhances academic outcomes but also contributes to the holistic development of students.

Implications for Teachers: The importance of classroom management extends to teacher effectiveness and professional satisfaction. Educators who master classroom management techniques often report higher levels of job satisfaction and lower levels of stress. A well-managed classroom allows teachers to focus on instruction rather than behavior management, leading to more enjoyable and rewarding teaching experiences.

In addition, effective classroom management skills can contribute to a **teacher's ability to implement innovative teaching strategies**, as they have the confidence that their classroom environment is conducive to learning. This professional growth can lead to better teaching practices and ultimately enhance student learning experiences.

Classroom management is a foundational component of the educational process that significantly impacts learning and student behavior. By establishing clear expectations, fostering a positive classroom climate, and addressing behavioral issues effectively, educators can create an environment where all students can thrive. The interconnectedness of classroom management, student engagement, and academic success highlights its importance in the teaching profession. As educators continue to develop their classroom management skills, they not only enhance their effectiveness but also contribute to the overall growth and development of their students.

Chapter 2

Understanding Classroom Management

> ***"What office is there which involves more responsibility, which requires more qualifications, and which ought, therefore, to be more honorable, than that of teaching?"***
>
> *— Harriet Martineau*

Classroom management is a vital aspect of effective teaching that involves a variety of **strategies and techniques aimed at creating an organized, respectful, and productive learning environment.** It encompasses everything from setting **rules and expectations to fostering positive relationships with students**. Understanding classroom management is essential for educators, as it significantly influences **student behavior, engagement, and overall academic success**.

The Foundations of Classroom Management: At its core, classroom management is about establishing a structured environment where students can learn effectively. This involves:

- **Setting Clear Expectations**: Teachers must communicate **clear rules and guidelines regarding behavior, participation, and academic integrity**. By outlining what is acceptable and what is not, educators create a sense of order and predictability within the classroom.

- **Creating Routines**: Consistent routines help students understand what to expect during class. **Routines for daily activities—such as entering the classroom, transitioning between tasks, and submitting assignments—minimize confusion and disruptions,** allowing for a more focused learning experience.
- **Establishing a Positive Climate**: A positive classroom environment **encourages respect, cooperation, and engagement**. Building rapport with students and creating a sense of community can foster a supportive atmosphere where students feel valued and are more likely to participate actively in their learning.
- **The Impact of Classroom Management on Student Behavior**: Effective classroom management directly influences student behavior. When expectations are clear and consistently reinforced, students are more likely to **comply with classroom norms**. Positive reinforcement strategies, such as praise and rewards for good behavior, can motivate students to engage in desirable actions. Conversely, addressing disruptive behavior promptly and fairly helps maintain respect and order in the classroom.

Moreover, a well-managed classroom reduces the likelihood of conflicts and distractions. By proactively identifying potential issues and implementing preventive measures, educators can create an environment that minimizes disruptions and maximizes learning time.

Enhancing Student Engagement and Learning: Classroom management is closely tied to student engagement. When students feel secure in their environment, they are more likely to participate actively in lessons and collaborate with their peers. Engaged students take ownership of their learning, leading to deeper understanding and retention of material.

Teachers can enhance engagement through various instructional strategies that cater to different learning styles. Incorporating **group work, hands-on activities, and technology can make lessons more dynamic and interesting,** further increasing student involvement.

The Role of Relationships in Classroom Management: Building strong relationships with students is a critical component of effective classroom management. When teachers demonstrate genuine interest in their students' lives and show empathy, they create an atmosphere of trust and respect. Students who feel connected to their teacher are more likely to adhere to classroom rules and engage positively in the learning process.

Additionally, fostering peer relationships among students promotes a collaborative classroom culture. **Encouraging teamwork and cooperation helps students develop social skills and enhances their overall educational experience.**

Professional Development and Continuous Improvement: Understanding classroom management is an ongoing process that requires professional development and reflection. Educators can benefit from training sessions, workshops, and peer observations that focus on effective management strategies. By continually refining their skills and approaches, teachers can adapt to the evolving needs of their students and classroom dynamics.

Understanding classroom management is essential for creating a productive learning environment. It involves setting **clear expectations, establishing routines, fostering positive relationships, and enhancing student engagement**. Effective classroom management not only minimizes disruptions and improves student behavior but also contributes to **academic success** and the overall well-being of students. As educators strive to create an optimal learning environment, their understanding of classroom management will be a key factor in shaping positive educational experiences and outcomes for all students.

"What is Classroom Management?"

Classroom management is the process by which **teachers create and maintain a productive learning environment in their classrooms.** It involves a **set of strategies and techniques designed to promote positive behavior, enhance student engagement, and facilitate effective learning.** A well-managed classroom allows educators to focus on instruction while ensuring that students feel safe, respected, and motivated to learn.

Key Components of Classroom Management

- **Establishing Rules and Expectations**: One of the foundational elements of classroom management is the establishment of clear rules and expectations. Teachers must communicate **what behaviors are acceptable** and what **consequences** may arise from misbehavior. This clarity helps students understand the boundaries within which they can operate, creating a structured environment that minimizes confusion and conflict.

- **Creating Routines**: Consistent routines are essential for effective classroom management. By implementing structured procedures for daily activities—such as entering the classroom, transitioning between tasks, and handling materials—**teachers can reduce downtime and keep students focused.** Routines help establish predictability, allowing students to navigate their learning environment with confidence.

- **Promoting Positive Relationships**: Building strong relationships with students is critical for effective classroom management. When teachers show genuine interest in their students' lives and create a sense of community, students are more likely to engage positively in the learning process. Strong teacher-student relationships foster trust, respect, and a supportive atmosphere where students feel valued.

- **Encouraging Engagement**: Engaging students in their learning is a key aspect of classroom management. Teachers can employ various instructional strategies—such as **group work, hands-on activities, and technology integration—to captivate students' attention and encourage**

participation. When students are actively involved, they are less likely to exhibit disruptive behaviors.

- **Addressing Behavior Issues**: Effective classroom management also involves the ability to address behavioral issues as they arise. Teachers must **be prepared to respond to disruptions with appropriate strategies that promote respect and understanding**. This can include redirecting student behavior, implementing consequences for misbehavior, and employing conflict resolution techniques.

The Impact of Classroom Management on Learning: The effectiveness of classroom management directly influences student learning and achievement. A well-managed classroom minimizes distractions and disruptions, allowing for more instructional time and greater student focus. Research has shown that classrooms with effective management practices tend to produce higher levels of student engagement and academic success.

Moreover, a positive classroom environment fosters **social-emotional development.** Students who feel safe and supported are more likely to take risks in their learning, ask questions, and collaborate with peers. This emotional security is crucial for developing resilience and a love of learning.

The Role of Professional Development: Understanding classroom management is an ongoing journey for educators. Professional development plays a significant role in equipping teachers with the **skills and strategies necessary for effective management**. Workshops, training sessions, and peer observations can provide valuable insights into successful practices, helping teachers refine their approaches and adapt to the diverse needs of their students.

Classroom management is a vital aspect of teaching that encompasses a range of **strategies** aimed at creating an effective learning environment. **By establishing clear rules, creating consistent routines, promoting positive relationships, and encouraging student engagement, educators can foster a classroom atmosphere conducive to learning.** Ultimately, effective classroom management not only enhances student behavior but also contributes to academic success, emotional development, and the overall quality of education. Understanding and implementing effective classroom management practices is essential for every educator seeking to make a positive impact on their students' learning experiences.

Teacher: *Why are you late for School?*

Student: *Because of a sign down the road.*

Teacher: *What do the sign have to do with being late?*

Student: *The sign said, "School Ahead. Go slow!"*

"Goals of Classroom Management"

(Creating a productive learning environment,
promoting positive behavior and maximizing instructional time.)

Effective classroom management is foundational to successful teaching and learning. It encompasses a variety of strategies aimed at achieving several key goals: creating a productive learning environment, promoting positive behavior, and maximizing instructional time. Each of these goals is interconnected and essential for fostering a space where students can thrive academically and socially.

Creating a Productive Learning Environment

- A productive learning environment is characterized by organization, **safety, and respect**. Achieving this goal begins with establishing clear rules and expectations that guide student behavior. When students understand what is expected of them, they are more likely to engage in positive behaviors and contribute to a respectful atmosphere.
- **Classroom layout** and organization also play a crucial role in productivity. A well-arranged classroom facilitates movement, collaboration, and access to resources, making it easier for students to engage with the material. Additionally, fostering an inclusive environment that values diversity helps students feel secure and supported, encouraging them to take risks in their learning.

Promoting Positive Behavior

- Promoting positive behavior is essential for maintaining a conducive learning atmosphere. Effective classroom management strategies include **using positive reinforcement, such as praise and rewards, to encourage desirable behaviors.** By acknowledging students' efforts and achievements, teachers can motivate them to continue demonstrating positive actions.

- Moreover, **addressing negative behaviors promptly and constructively is vital.** Implementing fair and consistent consequences for misbehavior helps students understand the **importance of accountability**. Techniques such as restorative practices can also be beneficial, as they focus on repairing harm and restoring relationships, rather than simply punishing students.

- **Creating a strong sense of community** within the classroom can further promote positive behavior. Activities that foster teamwork and collaboration encourage students to develop **social skills and empathy,** leading to a more respectful and supportive environment.

Maximizing Instructional Time

- Maximizing instructional time is critical for enhancing student learning outcomes. Effective classroom management ensures that **time spent in the classroom is focused on teaching and learning rather than on resolving conflicts or managing disruptions.** This can be achieved through the establishment of consistent routines that streamline transitions and minimize downtime.

- Engaging instructional strategies are also key to maximizing time. When lessons are interactive and tailored to students' interests and needs, students are more likely to be attentive and invested in their learning. Techniques such as **cooperative learning, hands-on activities, and technology integration can captivate students and keep them focused on the task at hand**.

- Additionally, **ongoing assessment and feedback** are essential for making the most of instructional time. By regularly evaluating student progress, teachers can identify areas where students may need additional support, allowing for targeted instruction that addresses individual learning needs.

The goals of classroom management: **creating a productive learning environment, promoting positive behavior, and maximizing instructional time**—are essential for fostering an effective educational experience. By implementing strategies that align with these goals, educators can cultivate a classroom atmosphere that supports student engagement and success. Ultimately, effective classroom management not only enhances learning outcomes but also contributes to the overall development of students, preparing them for future academic and social challenges.

"Philosophies of Classroom Management"

Classroom management is an essential component of effective teaching, influencing **student behavior, engagement, and overall academic success.** Various philosophies guide educators in their approach to managing classrooms, each reflecting different beliefs about teaching, learning, and student behavior. Understanding these philosophies can help educators develop their own strategies and create an environment conducive to learning.

Behaviorist Philosophy: The behaviorist philosophy is rooted in the idea that behavior is learned **through interactions with the environment**. This approach emphasizes observable behaviors and the use of reinforcement to shape student actions. In a behaviorist classroom, teachers set clear expectations and use rewards and consequences to encourage desired behaviors.

For example, positive reinforcement, such as **praise or tangible rewards**, can motivate students to adhere to classroom rules. Conversely, negative behaviors may be addressed through consequences. This philosophy is effective in promoting compliance and order but may not fully address the underlying reasons for certain behaviors. Critics argue that it can lead to extrinsic motivation rather than fostering intrinsic motivation for learning.

Constructivist Philosophy: In contrast to behaviorism, the constructivist philosophy emphasizes the role of students as **active participants in their own learning.** This approach views learning as a process of building knowledge through experiences and interactions. In a constructivist classroom, teachers create a **supportive environment** that encourages **exploration, collaboration, and critical thinking.**

Classroom management under this philosophy focuses on creating **opportunities** for student choice and autonomy. Teachers **facilitate** discussions, **encourage** group work, and provide hands-on activities that engage students in the learning process. The goal is to foster a sense of **ownership** over learning, promoting intrinsic **motivation** and a deeper understanding of the material. However, managing a classroom with high levels of student autonomy can be challenging and may require additional strategies to maintain order.

Humanistic Philosophy: The humanistic philosophy of classroom management prioritizes the emotional and social development of students. This approach is based on the belief that education should nurture the whole child, **focusing on personal growth, self-esteem, and interpersonal relationships.** In a humanistic classroom, teachers create a supportive and empathetic environment where students feel safe to express themselves.

Classroom management strategies aligned with this philosophy include building strong relationships with students, **fostering a sense of community, and encouraging open communication.** Teachers may use techniques such as conflict resolution and restorative practices to address behavioral issues, emphasizing understanding and personal responsibility. This approach can lead to a positive classroom climate, but it requires significant emotional investment from educators.

Democratic Philosophy: The democratic philosophy emphasizes the importance of **student voice and choice in the classroom**. This approach views education as a collaborative process where students actively participate in decision-making and governance. In a democratic classroom, teachers encourage students to contribute to the establishment of rules and norms, fostering a sense of ownership and responsibility.

Classroom management in a democratic setting involves creating opportunities for **students to express their opinions, engage in discussions, and participate in group decision-making.** This approach not only promotes positive behavior but also prepares students **for civic engagement and leadership**. However, achieving balance in a democratic classroom can be challenging, as it requires teachers to navigate diverse perspectives and opinions.

Culturally Responsive Philosophy: The culturally responsive philosophy of classroom management **recognizes and values the diverse cultural backgrounds of students**. This approach emphasizes the importance of understanding students' cultural contexts and incorporating these into the classroom environment. Culturally responsive educators strive to create an inclusive atmosphere where all students feel respected and valued.

Classroom management strategies within this framework include culturally relevant teaching practices, fostering positive relationships, and promoting equity. Teachers may adapt their approaches to align with the cultural norms and values of their students, thereby enhancing engagement and reducing behavioral issues. This philosophy promotes a sense of belonging and connection but requires educators to be continually reflective and responsive to the needs of their diverse student populations.

The philosophies of classroom management provide educators with diverse frameworks to guide their practices. Whether rooted in **behaviorism, constructivism, humanism, democratic principles, or cultural responsiveness**, each philosophy offers valuable insights into creating effective learning environments. By understanding and integrating these philosophies, educators can develop a comprehensive approach to classroom management that supports student engagement, promotes positive behavior, and fosters academic success. Ultimately, the effectiveness of any classroom management philosophy depends on the unique needs and dynamics of the classroom and the commitment of the educator to create a supportive and engaging learning environment.

"Different Approaches to Classroom Management: Assertive Discipline and Restorative Practices"

Classroom management is essential for creating a learning environment, and various approaches have emerged to help educators effectively manage student behavior and promote engagement. Two notable approaches are assertive discipline and restorative practices. Each approach offers distinct philosophies, strategies, and implications for teaching and learning.

Assertive Discipline

Overview

Assertive discipline is a behavior management approach developed by Lee Canter in the 1970s. This model emphasizes the importance of establishing clear rules and expectations while maintaining a strong, authoritative presence as a teacher. The fundamental premise is that teachers have the right to set boundaries and that students must be held accountable for their behavior.

Key Features

- **Clear Expectations**: Assertive discipline involves clearly defining rules and expectations at the beginning of the school year. Teachers communicate what behaviors are acceptable and what consequences will follow if those rules are broken.

- **Consistent Enforcement**: Consistency is crucial in this approach. Teachers must apply consequences fairly and consistently to reinforce accountability. This predictability helps students understand the importance of adhering to established rules.

- **Positive Reinforcement**: While the focus is on discipline, the approach also incorporates positive reinforcement for good behavior. Acknowledging and rewarding students who follow rules fosters a positive classroom climate and motivates others to comply.

Advantages

- **Structure and Order**: Assertive discipline provides a clear framework for managing behavior, helping to create a structured learning environment.
- **Accountability**: Students learn the importance of accountability for their actions, which can lead to improved behavior over time.

Challenges

- **Authoritarian Perception**: Some critics argue that the assertive nature of this approach can be perceived as authoritarian, potentially leading to resistance or fear among students.
- **Limited Focus on Relationships**: The approach may prioritize rules over the development of strong relationships, which are essential for fostering a positive classroom culture.

Restorative Practices

Overview

Restorative practices emerged as an alternative to traditional disciplinary approaches that often focus on punishment. This approach emphasizes repairing harm and restoring relationships rather than merely assigning consequences for misbehavior. Restorative practices aim to create a supportive and inclusive environment where students feel valued and respected.

Key Features

- **Focus on Relationships**: Restorative practices prioritize building strong relationships within the classroom community. Educators work to foster a sense of belonging among students, which can reduce the likelihood of disruptive behavior.

- **Inclusive Dialogue**: When conflicts arise, restorative practices involve open dialogue among all parties affected by the behavior. This includes the student who misbehaved, their peers, and the teacher. The goal is to understand the impact of the behavior and collaboratively determine how to repair any harm done.
- **Empathy and Accountability**: Restorative practices encourage students to reflect on their actions and consider how their behavior affects others. This emphasis on empathy fosters personal accountability and helps students develop problem-solving skills.

Advantages

- **Community Building**: Restorative practices promote a sense of community and belonging, which can enhance student engagement and cooperation.
- **Conflict Resolution**: This approach equips students with skills for resolving conflicts constructively, leading to better relationships and a more positive classroom environment.

Challenges

- **Time-Consuming**: Implementing restorative practices can be time-intensive, particularly during conflict resolution discussions, which may require careful facilitation.
- **Requires Training**: Teachers may need specialized training to effectively implement restorative practices, which can pose a challenge in terms of resources and support.

Both assertive discipline and restorative practices offer valuable frameworks for classroom management, each with its unique strengths and challenges. Assertive discipline emphasizes structure and accountability, providing a clear set of expectations for students. In contrast, restorative practices focus on building relationships, empathy, and community, aiming to repair harm and foster a positive classroom culture.

Ultimately, the effectiveness of any approach depends on the specific needs of the classroom, the dynamics of the student population, and the values of the educator. Many teachers find success in integrating elements from both approaches, creating a balanced management strategy that supports both discipline and relationship-building. By understanding and applying these different approaches, educators can create an environment that promotes positive behavior and enhances the overall learning experience for all students.

"Aligning Management Style with Personal Teaching Philosophy"

Effective classroom management is essential for fostering a productive learning environment, and aligning management style with personal teaching philosophy is a crucial aspect of this process. A teacher's philosophy of education reflects their beliefs about teaching and learning, influencing how they approach classroom management. When these elements are in harmony, it can enhance the educational experience for both teachers and students, leading to improved engagement, motivation, and academic success.

Understanding Personal Teaching Philosophy: A personal teaching philosophy encompasses an educator's beliefs about the nature of learning, the role of the teacher, and the importance of student agency. It can be shaped by various factors, including individual experiences, educational theories, and cultural backgrounds. Common philosophies include:

- **Constructivism**: This philosophy emphasizes active learning, where students build knowledge through experiences and interactions. Teachers adopting this philosophy often prioritize student-centered approaches that encourage exploration and critical thinking.

- **Humanism**: Focusing on the emotional and social aspects of learning, humanistic educators believe in nurturing the whole child. They prioritize relationships and create supportive environments that promote self-esteem and personal growth.

- **Behaviorism**: This philosophy emphasizes observable behaviors and the use of reinforcement to shape student actions. Teachers who adopt a behaviorist perspective may focus on setting clear rules and consequences to maintain order in the classroom.

Aligning Management Style with Teaching Philosophy

- **Consistency and Clarity**: For teachers who adhere to a behaviorist philosophy, consistency in management style is paramount. Establishing clear expectations and routines aligns with their belief in structured learning environments. This can involve setting explicit rules and using positive reinforcement to encourage desired behaviors, creating an atmosphere of accountability.
- **Student-Centered Approaches**: Educators with a constructivist philosophy often adopt a more flexible and collaborative management style. They may implement strategies that encourage student voice and choice, fostering a sense of ownership over the learning process. This alignment can include group work, project-based learning, and open discussions, allowing students to engage actively in their education.
- **Building Relationships**: For those who embrace a humanistic approach, relationship-building is central to their management style. Creating a nurturing environment where students feel safe to express themselves and take risks aligns with their belief in the importance of emotional well-being. Strategies may include restorative practices, regular check-ins, and fostering a classroom community that values empathy and respect.
- **Adaptability**: Acknowledging that students are diverse and that their needs may change is essential for all teaching philosophies. An effective management style should be adaptable, allowing educators to respond to varying dynamics within the classroom. This flexibility ensures that the management approach remains aligned with the evolving needs of students and the goals of the learning environment.

The Benefits of Alignment: When management style aligns with personal teaching philosophy, several positive outcomes can arise:

- **Enhanced Student Engagement**: A cohesive approach fosters a sense of belonging and motivation among students. When management strategies reflect the values inherent in the teaching philosophy, students are more likely to be engaged and invested in their learning.

- **Improved Classroom Climate**: An aligned management style contributes to a positive classroom climate where students feel respected and supported. This nurturing environment encourages collaboration, open communication, and mutual respect among peers.

- **Greater Teacher Satisfaction**: Educators who align their management style with their teaching philosophy often experience greater job satisfaction. When teachers feel authentic in their approaches, they are more likely to enjoy their roles and feel empowered to create meaningful learning experiences.

Aligning management style with personal teaching philosophy is vital for creating a productive and positive classroom environment. By reflecting on their beliefs about teaching and learning, educators can develop management strategies that support their philosophy and foster student engagement, motivation, and academic success. Whether adopting behaviorist, constructivist, or humanistic approaches, the key is to ensure that management practices are consistent with the underlying values and beliefs of the educator. Ultimately, this alignment enhances the educational experience for both teachers and students, creating a harmonious learning environment where everyone can thrive.

Chapter 3

Establishing a Positive Classroom Environment

> ***"Teach love, generosity, good manners and some of that will drift from the classroom to the home and who knows, the children will be educating the parents."*** *— Roger Moore*

Creating a positive classroom environment is essential for fostering student engagement, motivation, and academic success. A supportive and nurturing atmosphere not only enhances learning but also promotes social and emotional development. Here are key strategies for establishing a positive classroom environment.

Building Relationships: Strong relationships between teachers and students are foundational to a positive classroom environment. When students feel respected and valued, they are more likely to engage in learning. To build these relationships:

- **Get to Know Your Students**: Take time to learn about each student's **interests, strengths, and challenges**. This can be done through informal **conversations, surveys, or icebreaker** activities.

- **Show Empathy**: Demonstrate understanding and compassion towards students' experiences. **Acknowledge their feelings and provide support** when needed.

- **Encourage Open Communication**: Foster an atmosphere where students **feel comfortable expressing their thoughts and concerns**. Use strategies such as regular check-ins or suggestion boxes.

Establishing clear expectations: Clarity regarding rules and expectations is vital for maintaining order and promoting positive behavior. To effectively communicate these:

- **Set Specific Rules**: Develop a **set of clear, age-appropriate rules that outline expected behaviors.** Involve students in creating these rules to foster a sense of ownership.

- **Communicate Consequences**: Clearly explain the consequences for both positive and negative behaviors. This helps students understand the importance of their actions.

- **Consistent Reinforcement**: Apply rules consistently to ensure that all students are held to the same standards. Consistency builds trust and predictability.

Creating an inclusive atmosphere: An inclusive environment recognizes and values diversity, allowing all students to feel respected and accepted. To promote inclusivity:

- **Celebrate Diversity**: Incorporate diverse perspectives and materials into lessons. **Highlight different cultures, traditions, and experiences** to make all students feel represented.

- **Foster Collaboration**: **Use group work and cooperative learning strategies to encourage students to collaborate and learn from one another**. This builds community and understanding among peers.

- **Accommodate Different Learning Styles**: Differentiate instruction to meet the varied needs of students. Offering multiple ways to engage with content ensures that every student has the opportunity to succeed.

Encouraging Student Engagement: Active engagement is crucial for a positive learning environment. To keep students involved:

- **Use Interactive Teaching Methods**: **Incorporate hands-on activities, discussions, and technology** to make lessons dynamic and engaging.
- **Encourage Student Voice**: Give students opportunities to express their opinions and make choices about their learning. This autonomy fosters investment in their education.
- **Set High Expectations**: Challenge students **to strive for their best** while providing support and encouragement. High expectations can motivate students to excel.

Implementing positive reinforcement: Positive reinforcement can significantly enhance a classroom environment. To effectively encourage good behavior:

- **Acknowledge Positive Behavior**: **Regularly recognize and celebrate students' achievements and efforts**. This could be through verbal praise, rewards, or classroom shout-outs.
- **Create a Reward System**: Develop a system where students can earn points, privileges, or other incentives for demonstrating positive behaviors and meeting expectations.

Maintaining a Safe and Supportive Environment: A safe classroom is one where students feel secure both physically and emotionally. To create this atmosphere:

- **Establish Safety Protocols**: Clearly communicate safety procedures and ensure that students understand what to do in case of emergencies.
- **Encourage Respectful Interactions**: Foster an environment **where bullying and harassment are not tolerated**. Teach and model respectful communication and conflict resolution strategies.

- **Be Approachable**: Make sure students know that **you are available for support and guidance**. Being approachable encourages them to seek help when needed.

Establishing a positive classroom environment is crucial for enhancing student learning and well-being. **By building strong relationships, setting clear expectations, promoting inclusivity, encouraging engagement, implementing positive reinforcement, and maintaining a safe space, educators can create a nurturing atmosphere that supports academic success and personal growth**. A positive classroom environment not only benefits students but also contributes to a more fulfilling teaching experience.

"Creating a Welcoming Atmosphere for the Classroom"

A welcoming atmosphere in the classroom is crucial for fostering student engagement, motivation, and a sense of belonging. When students feel welcomed and valued, they are more likely to participate actively in their learning and develop positive relationships with peers and teachers. Here are key strategies for creating a welcoming classroom environment.

Inclusive Decor and Layout: The physical environment of the classroom plays a significant role in making students feel welcome.

- **Diverse Representation**: **Display materials and decorations that reflect the diversity of your students**. This can include **posters, books, and art from various cultures, promoting an inclusive environment** where all students see themselves represented.
- **Student Work Display**: Showcase student work prominently around the classroom. This not only honors their efforts but also gives students **a sense of ownership** over their learning space.
- **Comfortable Layout**: Arrange desks and seating **to facilitate collaboration and interaction**. A flexible layout that allows for group work and discussions creates a more inviting atmosphere.

Positive and Warm Communication: The way teachers communicate with students significantly impacts the classroom atmosphere.

- **Greet Students Daily**: Welcome students warmly as they enter the classroom. **A simple smile and greeting** can set a positive tone for the day.
- **Use Encouraging Language**: Foster a positive environment by using affirming language. Acknowledge students' efforts, **express enthusiasm for their ideas, and encourage them to take risks** in their learning.
- **Active Listening**: Show genuine **interest in students' thoughts and feelings**. Listening actively conveys that their voices matter, helping to build trust and rapport.

Establishing classroom norms together: Involving students in creating classroom norms helps foster a sense of community and belonging.

- **Collaborative Rule-Making**: At the beginning of the year, involve students **in establishing classroom rules and expectations**. This empowers them and creates a shared sense of responsibility for the classroom environment.

- **Discuss Values**: Engage students in discussions about respect, kindness, and cooperation. Highlight the importance of these values in building a welcoming community.

Creating a supportive community: Building a supportive classroom community enhances the sense of belonging among students.

- **Team-Building Activities**: Incorporate icebreakers and team-building exercises to help **students get to know one another**. These activities can break down barriers and promote friendships.

- **Peer Support Systems**: Encourage students to work together and support one another. Implementing buddy systems or collaborative projects fosters a sense of camaraderie.

Flexibility and Responsiveness: Being flexible and responsive to students' needs is key to maintaining a welcoming atmosphere.

- **Adapt to Individual Needs**: Recognize that **each student has unique strengths and challenges.** Be open to modifying lessons or providing additional support as needed to ensure all students feel included and capable.

- **Solicit Feedback**: Regularly ask for **student feedback** on classroom activities and norms. This not only empowers them but also helps you understand their perspectives and make necessary adjustments.

Celebrating Achievements and Milestones: Recognizing students' accomplishments fosters a positive and welcoming atmosphere.

- **Celebrate Successes**: Acknowledge both individual and group achievements, no matter how small. **Celebrating successes boosts morale** and motivates students to strive for excellence.
- **Mark Special Occasions**: Celebrate birthdays, cultural holidays, and significant milestones. These celebrations create shared experiences that strengthen community bonds.

Creating a welcoming atmosphere in the classroom is essential for promoting a positive learning environment. **By focusing on inclusive decor, positive communication, collaborative norm-setting, community-building, flexibility, and celebration of achievements, educators can foster a space where all students feel valued and engaged.**

"The Importance of a Safe and Inclusive Space in Education"

Creating a safe and inclusive space in educational settings is paramount for fostering effective learning and personal growth. Such an environment not only promotes academic success but also enhances **social and emotional well-being**. The significance of a safe and inclusive space can be understood through its impact on student engagement, mental health, social relationships, and overall educational outcomes.

Promoting Student Engagement

- A safe and inclusive classroom encourages active participation and engagement among students. When **students feel secure and accepted, they are more likely to express their thoughts, ask questions, and participate in discussions**. This engagement is critical for effective learning, as it fosters a sense of ownership over the educational process.
- In contrast, environments that are perceived as hostile or exclusionary can lead to disengagement and withdrawal. **Students who fear judgment or ridicule are less likely to take risks in their learning, ultimately hindering their academic progress**. By cultivating a safe space, educators empower students to contribute meaningfully, enhancing their overall learning experience.

Supporting Mental Health

- A safe and inclusive environment plays a vital role in promoting students' mental health. Schools are often where young people spend a significant portion of their time, making it essential for these spaces to be nurturing and supportive.
- When students feel safe from bullying, discrimination, or any form of harassment, their ability to focus on learning improves significantly. Conversely, an unsafe environment can lead to stress, anxiety, and depression, affecting students' academic performance and overall well-

being. Creating an inclusive atmosphere where every student feels valued and respected contributes to a sense of belonging, which is crucial for mental health.

Fostering Positive Social Relationships

- **Inclusion is a key factor** in building positive social relationships among students. A safe environment encourages **collaboration, cooperation, and understanding, allowing students to connect** with peers from diverse backgrounds.
- When students engage with one another in an inclusive setting, **they develop essential social skills, such as empathy, respect, and conflict resolution.** These skills are vital for personal development and future success in various social contexts. Moreover, inclusive spaces reduce the likelihood of bullying and social isolation, promoting a culture of respect and kindness.

Enhancing Academic Outcomes

- Research has shown that students who feel safe and included in their learning environments are more likely to achieve academic success. When **students are free from fear and feel valued, they can focus more on their studies, leading to improved performance and higher achievement levels.**
- Inclusion fosters **a sense of belonging**, which has been linked to increased motivation and perseverance in the face of challenges. Educators who prioritize creating safe and inclusive spaces empower students to set higher goals for themselves and work diligently to achieve them.

Encouraging Diversity and Equity

- A safe and inclusive space values diversity and promotes equity. By recognizing and celebrating the unique backgrounds, cultures, and perspectives of all students, educators create an environment that reflects the real world.

- This inclusivity prepares students for a diverse society, equipping them with the skills to navigate and appreciate differences. Moreover, it helps combat stereotypes and biases, fostering a more equitable society. Educators who actively promote inclusivity contribute to a culture of respect that extends beyond the classroom.

The importance of a safe and inclusive space in education cannot be overstated. Such environments enhance student engagement, support mental health, foster positive relationships, and lead to better academic outcomes. **By prioritizing safety and inclusivity**, educators create a foundation for personal growth and development, empowering students to reach their full potential. Ultimately, a safe and inclusive educational environment not only benefits individual students but also contributes to a more just and equitable society. As we continue to navigate an increasingly diverse world, the commitment to creating inclusive spaces in education remains essential for nurturing informed, compassionate, and engaged citizens.

"Strategies for Making the Classroom Physically Inviting"

Creating a physically inviting classroom is crucial for fostering a positive learning environment where students feel comfortable, engaged, and inspired. The layout, decor, and overall atmosphere can significantly influence students' attitudes toward learning. Here are several strategies to make your classroom more inviting.

Flexible Seating Arrangements

- **Varied Seating Options**: Incorporate different types of seating, such as bean bags, floor cushions, standing desks, and traditional chairs. This allows students to choose what works best for their learning style and comfort.
- **Collaborative Spaces**: **Create areas where students can work together** in small groups. Use movable furniture to allow for easy reconfiguration based on activities, encouraging collaboration and interaction.

Engaging Decor

- **Student-Created Art**: **Display artwork, projects, and other creations from students.** This not only personalizes the space but also instills a sense of pride and ownership.
- **Thematic Decor**: **Use themes that relate to the subjects being taught** or current events. This can make the classroom feel dynamic and relevant, sparking curiosity and interest.

Warm Colors and Natural Light: Use warm colors for walls and decorations to create a welcoming atmosphere. Ensure that natural light is maximized, as it positively affects mood and energy levels. Warm colors typically include:

- **Red**: Often associated with energy, passion, and action.
- **Orange**: Represents enthusiasm, creativity, and warmth.

- **Yellow**: Evokes feelings of happiness, positivity, and brightness.
- **Pink**: Often linked to love, compassion, and nurturing.
- **Peach**: A softer, inviting color that combines elements of orange and pink.
- **Coral**: A blend of orange and pink, symbolizing warmth and vibrancy.

These colors tend to create a sense of warmth and comfort, making them popular in design and decor to create inviting spaces.

Organized and Clutter-Free Environment

- **Effective Storage Solutions**: Use bins, shelves, and organizers to keep materials tidy and accessible. An organized space reduces distractions and makes it easier for students to find what they need.
- **Clear Zones**: Designate specific areas for different activities (e.g., reading corner, group work area, and quiet space). Clearly marked zones help students understand the purpose of each area and promote a sense of order.

Welcoming Entryway

- **Positive Messages**: **Create a welcoming bulletin board** at the entrance that features positive affirmations or greetings. This sets a positive tone as students enter.
- **Classroom Rules and Values**: Display classroom rules and values prominently to remind students of the expectations in a friendly and encouraging manner.

Interactive Learning Displays

- **Learning Stations**: **Set up interactive learning stations with hands-on materials related to the curriculum**. This invites students to engage actively with the content and explore at their own pace.

- **Showcase Learning Goals**: Use **visual aids to outline learning objectives** and ongoing projects. This keeps students informed and motivated, making the learning journey visible.

Comfort and Personal Touches

- **Personal Items**: Encourage students to bring in personal items or pictures that reflect their interests and identities. This not only makes the space feel more welcoming but also helps build community.

- **Cozy Reading Nook**: Create a **designated reading area with comfortable seating, soft lighting, and a variety of books**. This encourages students to relax and enjoy reading.

Incorporating Nature

- **Plants and Greenery: Add plants or flowers to the classroom** to enhance the atmosphere. Nature can have a calming effect and improve air quality.

- **Natural Materials: Use materials like wood, stone, or natural fibers** in the decor and furniture to create a warm and inviting environment.

Technology Integration

- **Interactive Displays**: Incorporate technology in an inviting way, such as **interactive whiteboards or tablets, to engage students** in innovative learning experiences.

- **Tech Stations**: Create **tech-friendly areas with charging stations** and organized cords to keep the space neat and functional.

By implementing these strategies, educators can create a physically inviting classroom that promotes a positive learning environment. A well-designed classroom not only enhances student comfort but also encourages engagement, collaboration, and creativity. Ultimately, when students feel welcome and valued in their learning space, they are more likely to thrive academically and socially. A thoughtfully arranged classroom sets the stage for a successful educational experience.

"Techniques for Fostering Rapport with Students"

Building rapport with students is essential for creating a positive and productive learning environment. When students feel a genuine connection with their teacher, they are more likely to engage, participate actively, and take risks in their learning. Establishing strong relationships also enhances students' emotional well-being and academic performance. Here are several effective techniques for fostering rapport with students.

Show Genuine Interest: One of the most powerful ways to build rapport is to show a genuine interest in students as individuals.

- **Learn Names Quickly**: **Addressing students by their names** makes them feel recognized and valued. Make an effort to learn their names within the first few days of class.
- **Ask About Interests**: Take time **to ask students about their hobbies**, interests, and aspirations. This not only demonstrates that you care about them personally but also helps tailor lessons to include topics they are passionate about.

Create a Welcoming Environment: A welcoming classroom atmosphere encourages students to feel safe and comfortable.

- **Positive Greetings**: Greet students **warmly as they enter the classroom.** A smile or a friendly word can set a positive tone for the day.
- **Inclusive Decor**: Use **classroom decorations that reflect the diverse backgrounds of your students**. This helps create a sense of belonging and shows that you value their identities.

Be Approachable and Available: Students need to know that they can come to you with questions or concerns.

- **Open-Door Policy**: Encourage students to approach you with any issues or inquiries, both academically and personally. Make it clear that your classroom is a safe space for dialogue.

- **Availability for Help**: Offer additional support outside of class time. Whether through office hours or informal check-ins, being accessible fosters trust.

Incorporate Humor and Positivity: A light-hearted approach can significantly enhance rapport.

- **Use Humor Appropriately**: Share **appropriate jokes or funny anecdotes** related to the lesson. **Humor can create a relaxed atmosphere** and make learning enjoyable.
- **Celebrate Small Successes**: Recognize and **celebrate students' achievements**, no matter how small. This fosters a positive environment where students feel motivated to contribute.

Engage in Active Listening: Active listening shows students that their opinions and feelings are valued.

- **Reflect and Respond**: When students share their thoughts or concerns, **reflect back what they've said and respond thoughtfully**. This demonstrates that you are fully engaged and care about their input.
- **Nonverbal Cues**: Use **eye contact, nodding, and open body language to convey attentiveness**. These nonverbal cues reinforce your commitment to understanding them.

Encourage Student Voice and Choice: Empowering students by giving them a voice fosters a sense of ownership in their learning.

- **Involve Students in Decision-Making**: Allow students to have **a say in classroom rules, activities, or project topics**. This inclusion fosters investment and accountability.
- **Flexible Learning Opportunities**: Offer **choices in assignments or learning methods**. When students feel they have control over their learning, they are more likely to engage deeply.

Be Authentic and Vulnerable: Being genuine fosters trust and reliability.

- **Share Your Experiences**: Share your own **learning experiences, including challenges and mistakes**. This helps students see you as a relatable figure, not just an authority.

- **Express Emotion**: it's okay to **show enthusiasm, passion, or even vulnerability when discussing topics**. Authenticity can inspire students to connect with you on a deeper level.

Build a Sense of Community: Creating a community in the classroom fosters connection among students and with the teacher.

- **Team-Building Activities**: Incorporate activities **that promote collaboration and teamwork.** These activities help students build relationships with one another and create a sense of belonging.

- **Peer Support Systems**: Encourage students **to support one another through buddy systems or group projects**. This strengthens social bonds and reinforces a positive classroom culture.

Fostering rapport with students is a vital aspect of effective teaching. By **showing genuine interest, creating a welcoming environment, being approachable, using humor, engaging in active listening, encouraging student voice, being authentic, and building a sense of community, educators can create strong connections with their students**. These relationships not only enhance the learning experience but also contribute to the overall emotional and social development of students. Ultimately, when students feel valued and connected, they are more likely to thrive academically and personally, leading to a successful and enriching educational journey.

"The Role of Trust in Effective Classroom Management"

Trust is a foundational element in effective classroom management. **When students trust their teacher and feel secure in their environment, they are more likely to engage, participate, and take risks in their learning.** Conversely, a lack of trust can lead to **disengagement, behavior issues, and a negative classroom atmosphere**. Understanding the role of trust in classroom management can help educators create a positive learning environment that fosters both academic and social-emotional development.

Building a Safe Learning Environment

- Trust creates a safe space for students to express themselves without fear of judgment or ridicule. **When students feel secure, they are more likely to participate actively in discussions, share their ideas, and ask questions**. This sense of safety is crucial for effective learning, as it allows students to take intellectual risks and explore new concepts without the fear of making mistakes.

- Educators can build trust by consistently **promoting a positive classroom atmosphere. This includes setting clear expectations for behavior, modeling respectful communication, and addressing conflicts or issues in a constructive manner.** When students see that their teacher is committed to creating a safe environment, they are more likely to reciprocate by adhering to the established norms.

Enhancing Student Engagement

- Trust directly influences student engagement. **When students trust their teacher, they are more inclined to invest emotionally and intellectually in their learning. Trust fosters a sense of belonging, which enhances motivation and participation**. Engaged students are more likely to contribute to discussions, collaborate with peers, and persevere through challenges.

- Teachers can enhance **engagement by showing genuine interest in their students' lives and learning. Taking the time to learn about students' interests, strengths, and challenges helps to build rapport and demonstrates that the teacher cares about their well-being.** This investment creates a positive cycle where students feel valued and are more likely to engage actively in their education.

Promoting Respect and Cooperation

- Trust is essential for fostering respect and cooperation among students. **When students trust their teacher, they are more likely to model that trust in their interactions with peers. A classroom built on mutual respect encourages students to collaborate, share ideas, and support one another.**

- To promote a culture of respect, educators should model respectful behavior and establish clear guidelines for communication. **Encouraging collaborative learning experiences and facilitating discussions about respect and cooperation helps students understand the importance of these** values in building a trusting community.

Facilitating Open Communication

- A trusting relationship between teachers and students promotes open communication. **When students feel they can speak openly about their thoughts, feelings, and concerns, they are more likely to share their struggles and successes.** This transparency allows teachers to address issues proactively and tailor their support to meet students' needs.

- Creating opportunities for **students to voice their opinions, provide feedback, and engage in dialogue fosters an environment where communication flows freely.** Regular check-ins, anonymous surveys, and informal discussions can help gauge student sentiments and reinforce that their voices are heard and valued.

Encouraging Accountability

- Trust is integral to fostering accountability among students. **When students trust their teacher, they are more likely to take responsibility for their actions and behaviors. A trusting relationship empowers students to acknowledge their mistakes and learn from them rather than fear punishment or judgment.**

- Educators can **promote accountability by setting clear expectations and providing consistent feedback**. When students see that their teacher believes in their ability to grow and improve, they are more likely to embrace responsibility for their learning and behavior.

"Building Resilience and Growth Mindset"

A trusting classroom environment encourages resilience and a growth mindset. When students trust their teacher, they feel supported in their efforts to overcome challenges. This support helps students develop resilience, allowing them to navigate obstacles with confidence.

Teachers can foster a growth mindset by emphasizing effort, perseverance, and learning from mistakes. By celebrating progress and encouraging students to view challenges as opportunities for growth, educators help students cultivate a resilient attitude that contributes to long-term success.

Trust plays a vital role in effective classroom management. By fostering a safe learning environment, **enhancing student engagement, promoting respect and cooperation, facilitating open communication, encouraging accountability, and building resilience, educators can create a positive atmosphere conducive to learning**. When trust is established, students feel secure and valued, leading to improved academic outcomes and social-emotional development. Ultimately, a trusting classroom environment benefits not only students but also educators, creating a dynamic and enriching educational experience for all involved.

Chapter 4

Setting Expectations and Rules

> ***"I saw as a teacher how if you take that spark of learning that those children have and you ignite it, you can take a child from any background to a lifetime of creativity and accomplishment."***
>
> *— Paul Wellstone*

Setting clear expectations and rules is a fundamental aspect of effective classroom management. When students understand what is expected of them, they are more likely to engage in positive behaviors that contribute to a productive learning environment. Establishing these guidelines helps create a sense of structure, promotes accountability, and fosters respect among students. Here are key strategies for effectively setting expectations and rules in the classroom.

Involve Students in the Process: One of the most effective ways to set expectations is to involve students in the rule-making process.

- **Collaborative Discussion**: Begin the school year by engaging students in a discussion about **what behaviors are important for a positive classroom environment.** Ask them what they believe should be included in the classroom rules.

- **Consensus Building**: Encourage students **to come to a consensus on a set of rules that everyone can agree on**. This inclusion fosters a sense of **ownership and responsibility** towards the classroom community.

Be Clear and Specific: Expectations should be articulated clearly and specifically to avoid any ambiguity.

- **Define Rules Clearly**: Use straightforward language to define each rule. For example, instead of saying "Be respectful," specify behaviors like "Listen when others are speaking" or **"Use polite language."**

- **Provide Examples**: Illustrate each rule with examples of both appropriate and inappropriate behaviors. This helps students visualize what is expected and understand the rationale behind each rule.

Communicate Consequences: Establishing consequences for both positive and negative behaviors is essential for accountability.

- **Positive Reinforcement**: Clearly **outline the rewards or recognition students** can earn for adhering to rules, such as praise, privileges, or points towards a class reward system.

- **Consequences for Misbehavior**: Communicate the **consequences for breaking rules in a calm and fair manner**. Ensure that students understand these consequences are not punitive but rather designed to help them learn from their mistakes.

Model Expected Behaviors: Teachers should model the behaviors they expect from students.

- **Demonstrate**: Actively demonstrate the expected behaviors during class activities. For example, show **how to engage in respectful conversations by modeling active listening.**

- **Consistency**: Consistently **uphold the rules and expectations in your own behavior, reinforcing the idea that everyone in the classroom, including the teacher,** is held to the same standards.

Create a Visible Reference: Having a visible reference for classroom rules can reinforce expectations.

- **Classroom Display**: Post the **rules in a prominent place in the classroom** where students can easily see them. This serves as a constant reminder of the agreed-upon expectations.

- **Regular Review**: Periodically **review the rules, especially at the beginning of each term or after breaks**, to refresh students' memories and reinforce their importance.

Establish a Routine: Routines help reinforce expectations and create a sense of stability in the classroom.

- **Consistent Procedures**: Develop and communicate specific procedures for common classroom activities, such as entering the room, turning in assignments, or transitioning between tasks. **Routines help minimize confusion and promote smooth operations.**

- **Practice**: Allow students to practice routines until they become second nature. **Rehearsing procedures helps solidify expectations and reduces disruptions.**

Encourage Reflection and Feedback: Encouraging students to reflect on their behavior and the classroom rules fosters personal accountability.

- **Regular Check-Ins**: Schedule regular check-ins where students can discuss how well they think the classroom is functioning and whether the rules are being followed.

- **Solicit Feedback**: Ask for student input on the rules and their effectiveness. This feedback can be valuable for making adjustments to better meet the needs of the classroom community.

Setting expectations and rules is a critical component of effective classroom management. By involving students in the process, communicating clearly, modeling behaviors, and establishing routines, educators create an environment conducive to learning and growth. **A well-structured classroom, grounded in mutual respect and accountability, not only enhances academic achievement but also fosters positive relationships among students and between students and teachers.** Ultimately, clear expectations and rules serve as the foundation for a successful and harmonious classroom community.

"Developing Classroom Rules"

Creating effective classroom rules is essential for fostering a positive learning environment where students feel safe, respected, and motivated to learn. Well-defined rules help establish clear expectations, promote positive behavior, and enhance classroom management. Here's a guide to developing classroom rules that work effectively.

Involve Students in the Rule-Making Process: Engaging students in the creation of rules fosters ownership and accountability.

- **Group Discussions**: Start with a class discussion about what a positive classroom looks like. **Ask students to share their ideas about behaviors that contribute to a respectful and productive learning environment**.
- **Consensus Building**: Encourage students to **suggest rules based on their discussions.** Aim for a consensus, ensuring that everyone feels heard and invested in the final rules.

Keep Rules Simple and Clear: Rules should be easy to understand and remember.

- **Limit the Number of Rules**: Focus on a small number of key rules—**typically 3 to 5**. This helps students remember them and reduces confusion.
- **Use Clear Language**: Write rules in straightforward language. For example, instead of saying "Maintain decorum," say "Use polite language."

Define Specific Behaviors: Make sure each rule specifies the behaviors expected from students.

- **Behavioral Examples**: Provide concrete examples for each rule. For instance, if a rule is "Be Respectful," you could define this as "Listen when others are speaking" or "Raise your hand to speak."
- **Positive Framing**: Frame rules positively to encourage desired behaviors. Instead of "Don't interrupt," say "Wait for your turn to speak."

Communicate Consequences: Clearly outline the consequences for both following and breaking rules.

- **Positive Reinforcement**: Explain how **following the rules will be rewarded**, such as through praise, class privileges, or a points system leading to rewards.
- **Consequences for Misbehavior**: Specify the **consequences for breaking rules in a constructive manner**. Ensure that students understand these are meant to help them learn and grow.

Make Rules Visible: Having a visual reminder of the rules can reinforce their importance.

- **Classroom Display**: Create **a poster or bulletin board displaying the rules prominently in the classroom**. This acts as a constant reminder for students.
- **Regular Review**: Periodically **review the rules, especially after breaks or when issues arise.** This helps keep expectations fresh in students' minds.

Model the Rules: Demonstrate the behaviors outlined in your rules to reinforce their importance.

- **Lead by Example**: As the teacher, model the expected behaviors consistently. **Show respect during discussions, actively listen, and follow the established rules yourself.**
- **Role-Playing**: Use **role-playing activities to demonstrate both the correct and incorrect ways to behave according to the rules**. This provides students with clear, relatable examples.

Encourage Reflection and Adaptation: Creating a culture of reflection helps students internalize the importance of the rules.

- **Class Discussions**: Hold regular discussions about how well the rules are working. Ask students for their input on whether any adjustments are needed.

- **Adjust as Necessary: Be open to modifying rules based on feedback and changing classroom dynamics.** Flexibility demonstrates that you value student input and are committed to creating the best possible learning environment.

Developing effective classroom rules is a collaborative process that sets the stage for a positive and productive learning environment. **By involving students, keeping rules simple and clear, providing specific behaviors, communicating consequences, making rules visible, modeling expected behaviors, and encouraging reflection, educators can create a classroom atmosphere that fosters respect, engagement, and accountability.** Ultimately, well-defined rules contribute to a harmonious classroom where students feel secure and motivated to learn.

"Importance of Clear, Concise, and Achievable Rules for Classroom Management"

Establishing clear, concise, and achievable rules is fundamental to effective classroom management. These rules serve as a framework that guides student behavior, fosters a positive learning environment, and promotes academic success.

Clarity in Expectations: Clear rules eliminate ambiguity, providing students with a concrete understanding of what is expected of them.

- **Guidance**: When students know exactly what behaviors are acceptable and what are not, they can **navigate classroom dynamics more confidently.** This clarity helps reduce confusion and misinterpretation of expectations.
- **Consistency**: Consistent enforcement of clear rules helps students feel secure in their learning environment. They understand that everyone is held to the same standards, which fosters fairness and equity.

Enhanced Student Accountability: Concise rules promote accountability among students by clearly outlining the behaviors that are expected.

- **Ownership**: When students understand the rules, they are more likely to take responsibility for their actions. This ownership fosters a sense of pride and commitment to maintaining a positive classroom atmosphere.
- **Self-Regulation**: Achievable rules empower students to self-monitor their behavior. When rules are realistic, students are more likely to adhere to them, leading to improved self-discipline.

Positive Learning Environment: Achievable rules contribute to a supportive and conducive learning environment.

- **Focus on Learning**: When rules are clear and concise, **students can focus on their learning rather than on navigating complex or unclear expectations**. This focus enhances engagement and participation.

- **Reduction of Disruptions**: Well-defined rules help minimize behavioral disruptions. Students are less likely to engage in inappropriate behavior when they clearly understand the consequences and expectations.
- **Promoting Respect and Cooperation:** Clear rules foster mutual respect and cooperation among students.
- **Shared Understanding**: When students collectively understand the rules, it promotes a sense of community. This shared understanding **encourages collaboration and respectful interactions.**
- **Conflict Resolution**: Clear rules provide a framework for addressing conflicts. When students know the guidelines, **they can resolve disputes more effectively,** referring back to the established expectations.

Facilitating communication: Concise rules improve communication between teachers and students.

- **Transparent Feedback**: When rules are well-defined, teachers can provide specific feedback to students regarding their behavior. **This transparency helps students understand the impact of their actions and promotes growth.**
- **Engagement in Rule-Making**: Involving students in the creation of rules can foster open dialogue. **When students have a voice in the process, they are more likely to buy into the rules and adhere to them.**

Supporting diverse learning needs: Achievable rules cater to the diverse needs of students in the classroom.

- **Tailored Expectations**: By **setting achievable rules, teachers can accommodate various learning styles and behavioral needs**. This approach ensures that all students can thrive within the established framework.
- **Gradual Implementation**: Rules **can be introduced gradually, allowing students to acclimate and adjust their behaviors over time**. This gradual approach supports students who may struggle with self-regulation.

The importance of clear, concise, and achievable rules in classroom management cannot be overstated. **Such rules provide clarity in expectations, enhance student accountability, promote a positive learning environment, foster respect and cooperation, facilitate communication, and support diverse learning needs.** By establishing a framework that is easy to understand and realistic, educators create an environment where students feel secure, engaged, and empowered to succeed. Ultimately, well-defined rules lay the foundation for a productive and harmonious classroom, benefiting both students and teachers alike.

> **"Teaching is not a lost art, but the regard for it is a lost tradition."**
>
> — *Jacques Barzun*

"Involving Students in the Rule-Making Process"

Involving students in the rule-making process is a powerful strategy for fostering a positive classroom environment. When students have a say in the development of rules, they are more likely to feel a sense of ownership and responsibility, leading to improved behavior and engagement.

Class Discussions: Start with an open dialogue about what a positive classroom environment looks like.

- **Brainstorming Sessions**: Hold a class meeting where students can share their thoughts on behaviors that contribute to a respectful and productive classroom. **Encourage all students to express their opinions and ideas**.
- **Guiding Questions**: Use specific questions to guide the discussion, such as "What do we need to feel safe in our classroom?" or "How can we support each other in our learning?"

Consensus Building: Once students have shared their ideas, work towards a consensus on the rules.

- **Prioritizing Ideas**: After gathering suggestions, have **students vote on the most important rules**. This helps to narrow down the list to a manageable number of clear expectations.
- **Compromise and Collaboration**: Encourage students to discuss and compromise on ideas to create rules that everyone can agree on. This **collaborative effort builds a sense of community and shared purpose.**

Drafting the rules together: After reaching a consensus, collaborate with students to draft the final rules.

- **Co-creation**: Invite students to help word the rules in a way that resonates with them. Their involvement in the language used will make the rules more relatable and memorable.
- **Visual Representation**: Consider creating a visually appealing display of the rules with student input. This could include drawings, posters, or a classroom contract that everyone signs.

- **Regular Reflection and Revision:** Make rule-making an ongoing process rather than a one-time event.
- **Check-Ins**: **Schedule regular check-ins throughout the school year** to discuss how well the rules are working. Ask students if they feel the rules are effective and whether they need adjustments.
- **Feedback Mechanism**: Create **an anonymous feedback system where students can share their thoughts on the rules without fear of judgment**. This allows for honest reflections and suggestions for improvement.

Empower Student Leaders: Encourage students to take leadership roles in enforcing and upholding the rules.

- **Classroom Jobs**: Assign roles to students, such as **"Classroom Monitors" or "Respect Ambassadors,"** who help remind their peers of the rules and model appropriate behavior.
- **Peer Support**: Create a system where **students can support each other in following the rules, fostering accountability among peers**.

Celebrate Success: Recognize and celebrate adherence to the rules as a class.

- **Recognition Programs**: Develop **a reward system that acknowledges** individuals or the entire class for following the rules. This could be through **verbal praise, certificates, or a points system leading to class rewards.**
- **Reflection on Achievements**: Regularly reflect as a class on how following the rules has positively impacted the learning environment. This reinforces the importance of the rules and encourages continued adherence.

Involving students in the rule-making process is an effective way to create a sense of ownership and responsibility in the classroom. **By facilitating discussions, building consensus, co-creating rules, reflecting on their**

effectiveness, empowering student leaders, and celebrating successes, educators can foster a collaborative classroom environment. This approach not only enhances student engagement and accountability but also contributes to a positive and respectful learning atmosphere where all students feel valued and empowered to succeed.

> **"You cannot teach a man anything; you can only help him find it within himself."**
>
> *— Galileo*

"Communicating Expectations in the Classroom"

Effectively communicating expectations is crucial for successful classroom management and fostering a positive learning environment. Clear expectations help students understand what is required of them, leading to improved behavior, increased engagement, and a more productive classroom atmosphere. Here are key strategies for effectively communicating expectations to students.

Be clear and specific: Clarity is essential when communicating expectations.

- **Use Simple Language**: Articulate expectations using straightforward, **age-appropriate language. Avoid jargon or overly complex terms that might confuse students.**
- **Define Specific Behaviors**: Instead of general statements like "Be respectful," specify behaviors, such as "Listen while others are speaking" or "Use polite language when giving feedback."

Model Expected Behaviors: Demonstrating expected behaviors helps reinforce expectations.

- **Lead by Example**: As the teacher, model the behaviors you expect from your students. **Show active listening, cooperation, and respect in your interactions.**
- **Role-Playing**: Engage students in role-playing activities where they can practice appropriate behaviors. This helps them visualize how to meet expectations in real situations.

Utilize Visual Aids: Visual representations can enhance understanding and retention of expectations.

- **Posters and Charts**: Create visually appealing posters that outline classroom expectations. Place them in prominent locations, such as near the entrance or on a classroom wall.

- **Visual Cues**: **Use symbols, icons, or color-coding to represent different expectations,** making it easier for students to grasp and remember them.

Incorporate Regular Review: Regularly revisiting expectations reinforces their importance.

- **Daily or Weekly Check-Ins**: Set aside time each week to review expectations with the class. This helps to remind students of the agreed-upon behaviors and their significance.

- **Feedback Sessions**: Encourage open discussions about how well the class is following the expectations. Solicit student feedback on what is working and what may need adjustment.

Provide Context and Rationale: Help students understand the reasons behind the expectations.

- **Explain the Importance**: Discuss why each expectation matters and how it contributes to a positive learning environment. Understanding the "why" helps students feel more invested in following the rules.

- **Connect to Goals**: Link expectations to larger classroom goals or values, such as respect, responsibility, or collaboration. This contextualization reinforces their relevance.

Encourage Student Ownership: Fostering a sense of ownership can enhance adherence to expectations.

- **Student Input**: Involve students in discussions about classroom expectations and the consequences for not meeting them. When students have a voice, they are more likely to feel accountable.

- **Classroom Agreements**: Collaboratively create a classroom agreement or contract that students can sign. This formalizes their commitment to upholding the expectations.

Use Consistent Language: Consistency in language reinforces clarity and understanding.

- **Reiterate Key Phrases**: Use specific phrases or terms consistently when discussing expectations. Repeating key phrases helps students internalize the language and makes it easier for them to recall.

- **Positive Reinforcement**: Use positive language when discussing behaviors. Instead of focusing on what not to do, emphasize what students should do instead.

Provide Ongoing Support and Guidance: Continual support helps students meet expectations effectively.

- **Individual Check-Ins**: Offer personalized support to students who may struggle with certain expectations. Regular check-ins can provide guidance and encouragement.

- **Recognize Improvement**: Acknowledge and celebrate when students demonstrate understanding and adherence to expectations. Positive reinforcement encourages continued compliance.

Communicating expectations effectively is a cornerstone of successful classroom management. **By being clear and specific, modeling behaviors, utilizing visual aids, incorporating regular reviews, providing context, encouraging student ownership, using consistent language, and offering ongoing support, educators can create an environment where students understand and embrace the expectations**. This clarity not only fosters a respectful and productive classroom atmosphere but also empowers students to take an active role in their learning and behavior. Ultimately, effective communication of expectations leads to a more harmonious and engaged classroom community.

"Strategies for Clearly Articulating Rules and Procedures"

Effectively communicating rules and procedures is essential for establishing a productive classroom environment. When students understand what is expected of them and how to navigate classroom routines, they are more likely to engage positively in their learning. Here are key strategies for clearly articulating rules and procedures:

Use Clear and Simple Language

- **Avoid Jargon**: Use straightforward language that is **age-appropriate**. This ensures that all students can easily understand the rules and procedures.
- **Be Specific**: Instead of vague statements, specify the exact behaviors or actions expected. For example, instead of saying "Be responsible," say "Turn in your homework by the end of the day."

Develop Visual Aids

- **Posters and Charts**: Create visually appealing posters that outline rules and procedures. Display them prominently in the classroom to serve as constant reminders.
- **Info graphics**: Use info graphics that illustrate steps in procedures (e.g., how to transition between activities) or outline rules in a visually engaging manner.

Model Procedures in Real-Time

- **Demonstration**: Act out or demonstrate the procedures in front of the class. For example, show how to line up quietly or how to ask a question during discussions.
- **Role-Playing**: Engage students in role-playing activities to practice procedures. This interactive approach helps reinforce understanding and retention.

Provide Written Documentation

- **Classroom Handbook**: Create a **classroom handbook** that includes all rules and procedures. Distribute it to students and parents at the beginning of the school year.
- **Checklists**: Provide **checklists for specific procedures, such as how to turn in assignments or how to participate in group work.** Students can refer to these documents as needed.

Incorporate Regular Review Sessions

- **Frequent Reminders**: Schedule regular check-ins or brief reviews of rules and procedures. This helps reinforce their importance and keeps them fresh in students' minds.
- **Reflection Activities**: Encourage students to reflect on their understanding of rules and procedures through discussions or written responses. This allows for clarification and adjustments if needed.

Use Consistent Language and Terminology

- **Standardized Phrasing**: Use consistent language when discussing rules and procedures. This repetition helps students internalize expectations.
- **Catchphrases**: Develop catchphrases or slogans related to specific rules (e.g., **"Respect others, respect yourself"**) to make them memorable.

Encourage Student Input

- **Collaborative Development**: Involve students in creating or refining rules and procedures. This collaborative approach increases buy-in and ownership.
- **Feedback Mechanism**: Create opportunities for students to provide feedback on the rules and procedures. This can help identify areas for improvement and foster a sense of community.

Utilize Technology

- **Digital Presentations**: Use slideshows or videos to present rules and procedures in an engaging manner. Visual media can enhance understanding and retention.

- **Classroom Management Apps**: Consider using classroom management tools or apps that allow for the easy sharing and referencing of rules and procedures.

Connect Rules to Real-Life Scenarios

- **Real-Life Examples**: Relate rules and procedures to **real-life situations** or classroom scenarios. This contextualization helps students see the relevance of the expectations.

- **Case Studies**: Discuss hypothetical situations where rules and procedures come into play, allowing students to think critically about their application.

Clearly articulating rules and procedures is vital for effective classroom management and student success. **By using clear language, developing visual aids, modeling procedures, providing written documentation, incorporating regular reviews, using consistent language, encouraging student input, utilizing technology, and connecting rules to real-life scenarios, educators can create a structured environment where students understand and adhere to expectations**. Ultimately, these strategies contribute to a positive and productive classroom atmosphere, enabling students to focus on their learning and development.

"Importance of Consistency in Enforcing Expectations"

Consistency in enforcing expectations is crucial for effective classroom management and fostering a positive learning environment. When rules and expectations are applied uniformly, it not only enhances student behavior but also builds trust and respect between teachers and students.

Builds Trust and Respect

- **Fairness**: When students see that rules are enforced consistently for everyone, they perceive the classroom as a fair environment. This fairness fosters trust between students and teachers, making students feel valued and respected.
- **Reliability**: Consistent enforcement allows students to know what to expect from their teacher. This reliability creates a stable environment where students feel safe and secure.

Encourages Accountability

- **Clear Consequences**: When expectations are enforced consistently, students understand that there are **clear consequences for their actions**. This understanding promotes accountability, as students are more likely to think twice before engaging in misbehavior.
- **Self-Regulation**: Knowing that rules will be applied consistently encourages students to **self-monitor their behavior**. They become more responsible for their actions, leading to improved self-discipline.

Reinforces Learning and Behavior Expectations

- **Clarity in Expectations**: Consistency helps reinforce what is expected of students. When rules are applied uniformly, students are more likely to internalize and adhere to those expectations over time.

- **Behavior Modification**: Consistent responses to both positive and negative behaviors can help modify student behavior effectively. When students receive immediate feedback for their actions, they learn to associate specific behaviors with consequences.

Reduces Confusion and Misinterpretation

- **Minimizes Ambiguity**: When expectations are enforced consistently, it reduces confusion about what is acceptable behavior. Students are less likely **to misinterpret rules or feel uncertain about how to act in various situations.**
- **Streamlines Classroom Management**: A consistent approach simplifies classroom management for teachers. It allows them **to respond to behaviors quickly and effectively, minimizing disruptions and maintaining a focused learning environment.**

Promotes a Positive Classroom Culture

- **Community and Cohesion**: A consistent approach to expectations fosters a sense of community within the classroom. Students feel that they are all held to the same standards, promoting a culture of cooperation and mutual respect.
- **Enhanced Motivation**: When students know that expectations are consistently enforced, they are more likely to engage positively in their learning. A stable environment enhances motivation and encourages students to participate actively.

Facilitates Effective Communication

- **Open Dialogue**: Consistency in enforcing expectations encourages open communication between students and teachers. Students feel comfortable discussing their behavior and understanding the rationale behind rules when they see them applied fairly.

- **Encourages Feedback**: When expectations are consistently enforced, students may be more willing to provide feedback on the classroom environment. This open line of communication can lead to positive changes and a more inclusive atmosphere.

Consistency in enforcing expectations is essential for creating a positive and productive classroom environment. **It builds trust and respect, encourages accountability, reinforces learning, reduces confusion, promotes a positive classroom culture, and facilitates effective communication**. By applying rules and expectations uniformly, educators can foster an atmosphere where students feel safe, respected, and motivated to learn.

Chapter 5

Routines and Procedures in the Classroom

> ***"You can teach a student a lesson for a day; but if you can teach him to learn by creating curiosity, he will continue the learning process as long as he lives."***
>
> *— Clay P. Bedford*

Establishing clear routines and procedures is essential for effective classroom management and fostering a positive learning environment. **Routines provide structure, while procedures outline specific steps for various tasks**. Together, they help students understand what to expect, minimize disruptions, and enhance engagement.

Importance of Routines and Procedures

- **Creates a Structured Environment**
  - Routines provide a predictable framework, helping students feel secure and focused. Knowing what **to expect reduces anxiety and helps students transition smoothly between activities.**
- **Enhances Efficiency**
  - Clearly defined procedures streamline classroom activities, allowing more time for learning. When students know how to complete tasks efficiently, **it minimizes downtime and maximizes instructional time**.

- **Promotes Independence**
  - Routines and procedures empower students to take responsibility for their actions. By teaching them how to navigate classroom tasks independently, educators foster **self-reliance and confidence.**
- **Reduces Disruptions**
  - Well-established routines help minimize behavioral disruptions. Students are less likely to engage in off-task behavior when they know the expectations and procedures for various activities.
- **Facilitates Classroom Management**
  - Routines provide a framework for classroom management, enabling teachers to maintain control and focus. Clear procedures reduce ambiguity and help manage student behavior effectively.

Implementing Effective Routines and Procedures

Identify Key Routines

- Determine the essential routines needed for daily operations, such as entering the classroom, transitioning between activities, and participating in group work.

Clearly Define Procedures

- For each routine, outline specific steps that students should follow. For example, for transitioning between activities, you might include steps like "Put away materials," "Raise your hand to speak," and "Wait quietly for instructions."

Model and Demonstrate

- Actively model each routine and procedure. Demonstrate the expected behaviors, showing students exactly what to do. This visual representation helps clarify expectations.

Practice and Rehearse

- Allow time for students to practice routines. Rehearsing procedures helps solidify understanding and builds confidence in carrying them out. Use role-playing or guided practice sessions for reinforcement.

Use Visual Supports

- Create visual aids, such as charts or posters that outline routines and procedures. Display them prominently in the classroom as constant reminders for students.

Provide Feedback and Reinforcement

- Offer constructive feedback when students follow routines and procedures correctly. Positive reinforcement, such as praise or rewards, encourages adherence to established expectations.

Review and Reflect

- Schedule regular reviews of routines and procedures. Discuss with students what is working well and what might need adjustment. This reflective practice fosters a sense of ownership and accountability.

Adapt as Needed

- Be flexible and willing to adapt routines and procedures based on the needs of your students. If a particular routine isn't working, seek student input and make necessary adjustments to improve effectiveness.

Examples of Common Routines and Procedures

- **Morning Arrival**
    - Students enter the classroom, hang up their belongings, and begin a morning activity or journal prompt.

- **Transitioning Between Activities**
  - Clear signals (like a bell or hand signal) indicate it's time to transition. Students know to finish their current task, put away materials, and prepare for the next activity.
- **Group Work**
  - Procedures for group activities include how to form groups, assign roles, and communicate with peers. Guidelines for sharing materials and time management can also be established.
- **Homework Submission**
  - A designated area for homework submission, along with clear instructions on how and when to submit assignments helps streamline the process.
- **Ending the Day**
  - Routines for packing up, reflecting on the day's learning, and preparing for dismissal creates a smooth end to the school day.

Routines and procedures are fundamental components of effective classroom management. **By establishing clear, consistent routines and well-defined procedures, educators create a structured environment that enhances learning, promotes independence, and minimizes disruptions. Through modeling, practice, and regular reflection, teachers can ensure that students understand and embrace these routines,** ultimately leading to a more productive and positive classroom experience.

"Importance of Daily Routines for Transitions and Tasks"

Establishing consistent daily routines for transitions and tasks is crucial for creating an **effective and positive classroom environment.** These routines not only help manage classroom flow but also contribute to students' emotional and cognitive development. Here are several key reasons why consistent daily routines are important:

Fosters Predictability and Security

- **Predictable Environment**: Consistent routines provide students with a sense of predictability. When students know what to expect throughout the day, it reduces anxiety and creates a stable learning environment.
- **Emotional Safety**: A predictable routine helps students feel safe and secure, enabling them to focus on their learning rather than worrying about what comes next.

Enhances Engagement and Focus

- **Minimized Disruptions**: Consistent transitions reduce the time spent on managing behaviors, allowing more time for learning. When students know the steps to follow during transitions, they can remain focused on tasks rather than becoming distracted.
- **Increased Participation**: Routines that are well-established encourage students to engage actively in activities. When students are accustomed to a routine, they are more likely to participate fully, knowing what is expected of them.

Promotes Independence and Responsibility

- **Self-Management Skills**: Daily routines teach students how to manage their time and responsibilities. By practicing these routines consistently, students develop independence and learn to take ownership of their actions.

- **Confidence Building**: Familiarity with routines fosters confidence. As students successfully navigate transitions and tasks, they build a sense of competence that positively impacts their overall learning experience.

Supports Efficient Use of Time

- **Streamlined Processes: Consistent routines make transitions smoother and quicker. This efficiency allows for more instructional time, maximizing the learning opportunities available to students.**

- **Less Time Wasted**: With established routines, teachers spend less time redirecting or managing behaviors during transitions, resulting in a more productive classroom atmosphere.

Encourages Positive Behavior

- **Clear Expectations**: Consistent routines communicate clear expectations for behavior during transitions and tasks. Students are more likely to follow guidelines when they understand what is required of them.

- **Reinforcement of Good Habits**: Repeated practice of routines reinforces positive behaviors. When students consistently follow routines, it helps establish good habits that contribute to a respectful classroom culture.

Facilitates Classroom Management

- **Reduced Stress for Teachers**: When routines are well-established, classroom management becomes easier. Teachers can focus on instruction rather than constantly managing transitions or student behavior.

- **Predictable Framework**: Routines provide a structured framework for the day, allowing teachers to plan lessons and activities more effectively while minimizing disruptions.

Encourages Social Skills Development

- **Cooperative Learning**: Consistent routines for group work or partner activities encourage collaboration and communication among students. This fosters social skills that are essential for teamwork and community building.
- **Conflict Resolution**: Routines that include steps for resolving conflicts or addressing issues help students learn how to navigate social interactions positively.

Consistent daily routines for transitions and tasks are essential for creating an effective and positive classroom environment. **They foster predictability, enhance engagement, promote independence, support efficient use of time, encourage positive behavior, facilitate classroom management, and aid in social skills development.** By implementing and maintaining these routines, educators can create a structured learning environment that benefits both students and teachers, ultimately leading to improved academic outcomes and a positive classroom culture.

"Creating a Structured and Supportive Classroom Environment"

Examples of effective routines (e.g., morning meetings, exit tickets)

Implementing effective routines can significantly enhance classroom management and foster a positive learning environment.

Morning Meetings

- **Purpose**: To build community, set a positive tone for the day, and outline expectations.
- **How It Works**: Each morning, students gather in a circle **to greet one another, share news, and discuss the day's agenda**. This routine encourages social interaction, reinforces classroom norms, and provides an opportunity for students to express themselves.

Classroom Jobs

- **Purpose**: To promote responsibility and ownership among students.
- **How It Works**: Assign specific roles (e.g., line leader, materials manager, tech helper) to students each week or month. Rotating these jobs helps students develop various skills and fosters a sense of community and teamwork.

Transitions between activities

- **Purpose**: To ensure **smooth movement from one activity to another**.
- **How It Works**: Establish a clear signal (like a chime or hand signal) to indicate transitions. Provide specific steps for transitioning, such as "Finish your last sentence, put away materials, and line up quietly." Practice this routine regularly to enhance efficiency.

Exit Tickets

- **Purpose**: To assess student understanding and gather feedback.
- **How It Works**: At the end of a lesson, students complete a brief written response to questions such as "What did you learn today?" or "What questions do you still have?" This routine allows teachers to gauge comprehension and adjust future lessons accordingly.

Weekly Reflection Journals

- **Purpose**: To encourage self-assessment and reflection on learning.
- **How It Works**: Set aside time each week for students to write in reflection journals. They can summarize what they learned, set goals for the next week, or express their thoughts about classroom activities. This routine fosters metacognition and personal growth.

Learning Stations

- **Purpose**: To promote active learning and engagement.
- **How It Works**: Organize the classroom into different learning stations, each focusing on a specific skill or concept. Students rotate through the stations at timed intervals, engaging in hands-on activities. Clear procedures for moving between stations help maintain order.

Classroom Norms Review

- **Purpose**: To reinforce classroom expectations and norms.
- **How It Works**: Regularly schedule time (e.g., weekly or monthly) to review classroom norms. Use discussions, role-plays, or games to engage students in understanding and practicing these norms, reinforcing their importance in daily interactions.

Mindfulness or calm down time

- **Purpose**: To promote emotional regulation and focus.
- **How It Works**: Set aside a few minutes each day for mindfulness activities, such as deep breathing, guided visualization, or quiet reading. This routine helps students center themselves and prepares them for learning.

Homework Check-in

- **Purpose**: To ensure accountability and support.
- **How It Works**: Begin class with a quick check-in on homework completion. Students can share what they found challenging or interesting. This routine encourages accountability and allows for immediate support where needed.

End-of-Day Review

- **Purpose**: To summarize the day's learning and prepare for the next day.
- **How It Works**: At the end of each day, dedicate a few minutes for students to share what they learned, ask questions, or set goals for the next day. This routine reinforces learning and helps students transition smoothly to dismissal.

Effective **routines, such as morning meetings, classroom jobs, transitions, exit tickets, weekly reflections, learning stations, norms review, mindfulness time, homework check-ins, and end-of-day reviews, play a vital role in creating a structured and supportive classroom environment.** By incorporating these routines, educators can enhance student engagement, promote responsibility, and facilitate a positive learning atmosphere that benefits all students.

"Teaching Procedures: Establishing Effective Classroom Routines"

Teaching procedures are essential components of effective classroom management and instructional practice. **They provide students with clear expectations on how to perform specific tasks, navigate transitions, and engage in classroom activities. Well-defined procedures not only promote a productive learning environment but also enhance student independence and accountability.**

Importance of Teaching Procedures

- **Clarity and Structure**: Teaching procedures give students a clear understanding of what is expected of them. **By outlining specific steps for various tasks, teachers can minimize ambiguity, helping students know exactly how to behave and what to do in different situations.** This clarity fosters a structured learning environment where students feel secure and focused.

- **Promotes Independence**: When procedures are taught explicitly, students become more capable of managing their own learning. **They learn how to follow directions and complete tasks independently, which builds confidence and self-efficacy**. Over time, this independence contributes to their overall academic success and personal development.

- **Enhances Classroom Efficiency**: Well-defined procedures streamline classroom activities, allowing for smoother transitions and more efficient use of instructional time. By reducing time spent on managing behaviors or explaining tasks repeatedly, teachers can dedicate more time to teaching and learning.

- **Reduces Disruptions**: Consistent procedures help prevent behavioral disruptions by providing students with a clear framework for their actions. When students know what to expect and how to respond, they are less likely to engage in off-task behavior or misunderstand classroom expectations.

- **Encourages Positive Behavior**: Teaching procedures fosters a culture of accountability. When students understand the procedures and the reasons behind them, they are more likely to adhere to the established norms, promoting a respectful and collaborative classroom atmosphere.

Key Elements of Effective Teaching Procedures

- **Clarity: Procedures should be articulated clearly and concisely. Teachers need to use simple language and avoid jargon that may confuse students. Each procedure should outline specific steps that students need to follow.**

- **Modeling**: Demonstrating the expected behaviors is crucial. Teachers should model each procedure, showing students how to perform tasks correctly. **This modeling helps students visualize what is expected and reinforces their understanding.**

- **Practice and Rehearsal**: Students should have opportunities to practice the procedures. **Rehearsing routines and tasks helps solidify understanding and ensures that students feel confident in their abilities** to follow the procedures.

- **Visual Supports**: Utilizing **visual aids, such as charts or posters, can enhance students' understanding of procedures**. Displaying these visuals in the classroom serves as a constant reminder of expectations and steps involved in various tasks.

- **Feedback and Reinforcement**: Providing feedback when students successfully follow procedures is essential. Positive reinforcement encourages adherence to established norms and helps students recognize the value of following procedures.

- **Regular Review**: Routines should be **revisited regularly** to ensure that students remain familiar with them. Periodic reviews provide opportunities for discussion, reflection, and adjustments as needed.

Strategies for Implementing Teaching Procedures

- **Establish a Routine for Each Activity**: Develop specific routines for daily activities, such as entering the classroom, transitioning between lessons, and participating in group work. For example, create a consistent process for how students should hand in homework or prepare for a test.

- **Use Consistent Language**: Employ the same phrases or terms when discussing procedures. This consistency helps reinforce understanding and makes it easier for students to recall the procedures.

- **Involve Students in the Process**: Engaging students in discussions about procedures can promote ownership and accountability. Involving them in creating classroom norms or procedures encourages a sense of community and respect for the established guidelines.

- **Integrate Procedures into Lessons**: When introducing new content, take time to teach and practice the procedures associated with that lesson. For instance, if students are working on a group project, explicitly outline the procedures for group collaboration.

- **Utilize Technology**: Consider using digital tools to reinforce procedures. Online platforms can provide visual representations of procedures, instructional videos, or interactive checklists that students can refer to as needed.

Teaching procedures is a fundamental aspect of effective classroom management and instructional practice. **By establishing clear, structured routines, educators create an environment conducive to learning and personal growth. Teaching procedures not only enhances student independence and accountability but also promotes a positive classroom culture**. Through modeling, practice, visual supports, and regular review, teachers can ensure that students understand and embrace these procedures, leading to improved academic outcomes and a harmonious learning atmosphere. Ultimately, effective teaching procedures lay the groundwork for successful learning experiences that benefit all students.

"Techniques for Explicitly Teaching Classroom Procedures"

Explicitly teaching classroom procedures is vital for establishing a well-managed learning environment. When students understand how to navigate various tasks and transitions, they are more likely to engage positively and focus on their learning.

Modeling

- **Demonstrate the Procedure**: Teachers should model each procedure step-by-step. For instance, if teaching how to transition between activities, the teacher can show how to put materials away, line up, and wait quietly.
- **Think Aloud**: While modeling, verbalize thoughts to provide insight into the decision-making process. This helps students understand not just what to do, but why each step is important.

Guided Practice

- **Practice Together**: After modeling, involve students in practicing the procedure as a group. For example, during a fire drill, walk through the exit route together, emphasizing each step.
- **Provide Support**: Offer guidance and corrective feedback during practice sessions to ensure students understand the expectations. Encourage students to ask questions if they are unsure about any part of the procedure.

Visual Aids

- **Create Visual Supports**: Develop posters, charts, or info graphics that outline each procedure. Use visuals to illustrate the steps clearly, making it easier for students to reference when needed.
- **Display Prominently**: Place visual aids in strategic locations around the classroom where students can easily see them, such as near the entrance or above their workstations.

Role-Playing

- **Simulate Scenarios**: Engage students in role-playing activities where they can practice procedures in a controlled setting. For example, have them practice how to ask for help or how to work collaboratively in a group.
- **Peer Modeling**: Encourage students to model procedures for their peers. This not only reinforces the procedure but also allows students to learn from each other.

Checklists and Step-by-Step Guides

- **Develop Checklists**: Create **checklists that outline the steps** involved in various procedures, such as turning in assignments or preparing for a presentation. Students can use these checklists to ensure they follow all steps correctly.
- **Distribute Guides**: Provide **written step-by-step guides** for complex tasks, ensuring that students have a resource to refer to as they practice.

Regular Review and Reinforcement

- **Schedule Review Sessions**: Regularly revisit procedures to reinforce understanding. This can be done through quick refreshers at the start of a lesson or dedicated review days.
- **Positive Reinforcement**: **Acknowledge and reward students** who follow procedures correctly. Use praise, stickers, or other incentives to encourage adherence to established norms.

Feedback and Reflection

- **Provide Constructive Feedback**: After students practice a procedure, offer feedback on their performance. Highlight what they did well and areas for improvement.
- **Encourage Reflection**: Have students reflect on their experiences with the procedure. This could be done through discussions or written reflections, helping them internalize the importance of following procedures.

Use Technology

- **Incorporate Multimedia**: Utilize videos or interactive presentations to demonstrate procedures. Visual learning can be particularly effective for students who benefit from seeing processes in action.
- **Digital Checklists**: Consider using classroom management apps that allow students to access digital checklists or reminders for procedures, making it easier for them to stay organized.

Involve Students in Creating Procedures

- **Collaborative Development**: Involve students in the process of creating procedures. This can foster ownership and buy-in, as they feel invested in the rules and routines of the classroom.
- **Discussion and Feedback**: Encourage students to provide input on the effectiveness of existing procedures. This can help identify areas for improvement and adapt routines to better meet their needs.

Explicitly teaching classroom procedures is essential for fostering a productive learning environment. **By employing techniques such as modeling, guided practice, visual aids, role-playing, checklists, regular review, feedback, technology integration, and student involvement, educators can ensure that students understand and adhere to established routines**. This clarity not only enhances student engagement and independence but also contributes to a positive classroom culture where learning can thrive.

"Reinforcement and Practice to Ensure Understanding of Classroom Procedures"

Reinforcement and practice are critical components in ensuring that students understand and can effectively follow classroom procedures. These strategies help solidify learning, promote consistency in behavior, and foster a positive classroom environment.

Consistent Reinforcement

- **Positive Reinforcement**: Recognize and reward students who follow procedures correctly. Use verbal praise, stickers, or small rewards to reinforce desirable behavior. For example, acknowledging a student who transitions smoothly between activities can encourage others to do the same.
- **Behavioral Contracts**: Create agreements with students outlining expectations for following procedures. Involve students in setting goals and provide incentives for meeting those goals over a specified period.

Frequent Practice

- **Scheduled Practice Sessions**: Incorporate regular practice of procedures into the daily or weekly schedule. For instance, take time at the beginning of each week to review and practice routines, such as entering the classroom or lining up for recess.
- **Mock Scenarios**: Create scenarios where students can practice procedures in context. For example, simulate a classroom discussion or a group project, allowing students to apply the procedures in a real-world setting.

Use of Visual Aids

- **Visual Reminders**: Display charts or posters that outline key procedures in visible areas of the classroom. These visual aids serve as constant reminders and help reinforce the steps involved in each procedure.

- **Interactive Displays**: Consider using bulletin boards or digital screens that change periodically to highlight specific procedures, keeping the information fresh and relevant.

Peer Teaching

- **Student Demonstrations**: **Encourage students to teach their peers about specific procedures.** This not only reinforces the knowledge for the student demonstrating but also provides additional perspectives and explanations for others.
- **Buddy Systems**: **Pair students to help each other with following procedures.** This peer support can create accountability and foster collaboration while reinforcing the procedures in practice.

Feedback Loops

- **Constructive Feedback**: After practice sessions, provide specific feedback to students about their performance. Highlight what they did well and offer suggestions for improvement, ensuring they understand how to refine their actions.
- **Self-Assessment**: Encourage **students to reflect on their adherence to procedures.** After practicing, have them evaluate their own performance and identify areas where they can improve.

Games and Activities

- **Incorporate Fun**: Use games and interactive activities to practice procedures. For example, create a quiz or a role-playing game that allows students to engage with the procedures in a dynamic way.
- **Challenge Formats**: Organize friendly competitions where students are rewarded for demonstrating proper procedures in various contexts, such as a timed transition or effective collaboration during group work.

Regular Review Sessions

- **Routine Refreshers**: Schedule periodic review sessions for classroom procedures. These could be **brief, 5-10 minute sessions** where you go over the procedures, discuss any changes, and allow students to ask questions.
- **Reflection Circles**: Use **group discussions to reflect on the effectiveness of procedures**. Ask students what they think is working well and what could be improved, allowing them to take ownership of their learning environment.

Integration into Daily Activities

- **Embedding Procedures**: Integrate procedures into daily lessons and activities. For instance, if students are learning about teamwork, explicitly discuss and practice the procedures for effective group collaboration during the lesson.
- **Routine Integration**: Make following procedures part of the **daily rhythm**, such as consistently using a specific signal to indicate when it's time to quiet down or transition to a new task.

Reinforcement and practice are vital in ensuring that students understand and can effectively follow classroom procedures. **By employing strategies such as consistent reinforcement, frequent practice, visual aids, peer teaching, feedback loops, games, regular reviews, and integration into daily activities, educators can create a supportive learning environment that promotes accountability and fosters student independence**. These efforts not only enhance students' understanding of procedures but also contribute to a positive classroom culture where all students can thrive.

Chapter 6

Monitoring and Observing Student Behavior

> ***"Most of us end up with no more than five or six people who remember us. Teachers have thousands of people who remember them for the rest of their lives."***
>
> *— Andy Rooney*

Monitoring and observing student behaviors are critical components of effective classroom management. By actively engaging in these practices, teachers can gain valuable insights into student interactions, learning processes, and the overall classroom environment.

Importance of Monitoring and Observing Student Behavior

- **Identifying Learning Needs**: Observations help teachers identify individual and group learning needs. **By noting how students engage with tasks, interact with peers, and respond to instruction, teachers can tailor their approaches to meet diverse needs.**

- **Enhancing Classroom Management**: Regular monitoring allows teachers to detect potential disruptions early. **By observing student behavior, educators can intervene before issues escalate, maintaining a positive classroom atmosphere.**

- **Fostering Engagement**: By observing how students respond to various activities, teachers can gauge engagement levels. Understanding what captures students' interest enables educators to adapt lessons and create more engaging learning experiences.
- **Building Relationships**: Consistent monitoring helps teachers build rapport with students. **By being attentive to their behaviors and needs, educators demonstrate care and concern, fostering a supportive classroom environment.**
- **Informing Instructional Decisions**: Observations provide real-time data that can inform instructional strategies. Teachers can modify their lessons based on what they see, ensuring that teaching approaches align with student responses and needs.

Techniques for Monitoring and Observing Student Behavior

Anecdotal Records

- **Description**: **Keep brief, descriptive notes about specific student behaviors during lessons or activities**.
- **Application**: Use these records to track patterns over time, helping identify students who may need additional support or intervention.

Checklists and Rating Scales

- **Description**: Develop checklists or rating scales to systematically observe and record specific behaviors.
- **Application**: Use these tools during group activities or transitions to assess how well students are following procedures or collaborating with peers.

Structured Observations

- **Description**: Set specific goals for what to observe during a lesson. For example, focus on student participation, interaction quality, or adherence to classroom procedures.

- **Application**: Use a structured observation form to guide your notes and ensure consistency in what is being observed.

Peer Observations

- **Description**: Collaborate with colleagues to observe each other's classrooms. This can provide new perspectives and insights.
- **Application**: Use feedback from peers to reflect on your practices and identify areas for improvement.

Self-Monitoring

- **Description**: Encourage students to engage in self-monitoring by reflecting on their own behaviors and learning.
- **Application**: Implement journals or reflection sheets where students can record their thoughts about their participation and behavior.

Behavioral Interventions

- **Description**: Implement specific behavioral interventions based on observations.
- **Application**: For example, if a student frequently disrupts class, create a behavior plan that includes monitoring and support strategies tailored to that student's needs.

Classroom Technology

- **Description**: Utilize classroom management software or apps to track student behavior and engagement.
- **Application**: Many tools provide real-time data and analytics, helping teachers identify trends and adjust their strategies accordingly.

Benefits of Monitoring and Observing Student Behavior

- **Improved Student Outcomes**: By closely monitoring behavior, teachers can identify and address learning gaps, leading to better academic performance and social-emotional development.

- **Enhanced Classroom Climate**: Proactive monitoring helps create a positive classroom environment, where students feel supported and understood. This atmosphere encourages collaboration and respectful interactions.

- **Informed Professional Development**: Observations can highlight areas for professional growth. Teachers can use insights gained from monitoring to seek targeted professional development opportunities.

- **Stronger Relationships**: Regular observation fosters deeper connections between teachers and students. When educators demonstrate that they are attentive and responsive to student needs, it builds trust and rapport.

- **Increased Engagement**: By adapting lessons based on observed engagement levels, teachers can create more dynamic and responsive learning experiences, enhancing student interest and participation.

Monitoring and observing student behaviors are vital practices for effective classroom management and instructional improvement. **Through techniques such as anecdotal records, checklists, structured observations, peer feedback, and technology, educators can gain valuable insights into student needs and engagement levels. The benefits of these practices extend beyond academic outcomes; they foster a positive classroom climate, strengthen relationships, and inform instructional strategies**. Ultimately, by prioritizing observation and monitoring, teachers can create an environment that supports all students in reaching their full potential.

"In learning you will teach, and in teaching you will learn."

— Phil Collins

"Proactive Monitoring: Enhancing Classroom Management and Student Success"

Proactive monitoring is an essential strategy in effective classroom management that involves anticipating and addressing student behavior and learning needs before they escalate into issues. **By actively observing and engaging with students, educators can create a supportive learning environment that fosters academic success and positive behavior.**

Significance of Proactive Monitoring

- **Prevention of Disruptions**: By observing student behavior closely, teachers can identify potential disruptions before they occur. This foresight allows for timely interventions, reducing the likelihood of classroom chaos and maintaining a focused learning environment.
- **Tailoring Instruction**: Proactive monitoring helps teachers assess student understanding and engagement in real time. This enables educators to adjust their instructional strategies and materials to better meet the needs of their students.
- **Building Relationships**: When teachers actively engage with students and monitor their progress, they demonstrate care and investment in their learning. This fosters stronger relationships and a sense of community within the classroom.
- **Encouraging Self-Regulation**: By modeling proactive monitoring, teachers can help students develop self-monitoring skills. This empowers students to recognize their own behaviors and take responsibility for their actions.

Techniques for Proactive Monitoring

- **Frequent Circulation**: Teachers should move around the classroom regularly during lessons. This physical presence allows them to observe student interactions and engagement levels closely. It also sends a message that the teacher is available for support.

- **Check-Ins**: Implement regular check-ins with students, either individually or in small groups. These brief interactions can provide insights into students' understanding, feelings, and any challenges they may be facing.
- **Use of Nonverbal Signals**: Employ nonverbal cues, such as eye contact, gestures, or subtle prompts, to gauge student engagement. Observing students' body language can provide valuable information about their focus and emotional state.
- **Classroom Management Tools**: Utilize technology or classroom management software that allows for real-time tracking of student behavior and engagement. These tools can help identify patterns and trends that may require attention.
- **Establishing Clear Expectations**: Clearly communicate classroom expectations and procedures from the beginning. This clarity allows students to understand what is required of them, making it easier for teachers to monitor compliance.
- **Behavioral Data Collection**: Collect data on student behavior and academic performance regularly. This could involve tracking participation, assignment completion, or instances of disruptive behavior to identify trends that need addressing.
- **Creating a Positive Environment**: Foster a classroom culture that emphasizes respect, collaboration, and support. A positive environment encourages students to engage meaningfully and reduces the likelihood of disruptive behaviors.

Benefits of Proactive Monitoring

- **Improved Student Engagement**: By addressing issues before they escalate, proactive monitoring helps maintain high levels of student engagement and motivation, leading to better academic outcomes.

- **Reduced Behavioral Issues**: Anticipating and addressing potential disruptions minimizes behavioral problems, allowing for a more focused and productive classroom atmosphere.
- **Informed Instruction**: Regular monitoring provides valuable data that can inform instructional decisions, enabling teachers to tailor their lessons to better meet the needs of their students.
- **Enhanced Student Self-Efficacy**: When students feel supported and understood, they are more likely to take ownership of their learning. Proactive monitoring fosters a sense of accountability and encourages self-regulation.
- **Stronger Classroom Community**: Proactive monitoring promotes positive relationships between teachers and students, creating a sense of community where everyone feels valued and supported.

Proactive monitoring is a crucial strategy for effective classroom management that enhances student success and fosters a positive learning environment. **By employing techniques such as frequent circulation, regular check-ins, and clear communication of expectations, educators can anticipate and address student needs before issues arise. The benefits of proactive monitoring extend beyond academic performance; they contribute to stronger relationships, increased student engagement, and a supportive classroom community**. Ultimately, by prioritizing proactive monitoring, teachers can create an environment where all students can thrive.

"Strategies for Circulating the Classroom and Engaging with Students"

Effective classroom circulation and engagement are vital for fostering a positive learning environment. When teachers actively circulate the classroom, they can observe student interactions, provide support, and build relationships. Here are several strategies for effectively circulating the classroom and engaging with students:

Purposeful Movement

- **Plan your Circulation**: Have a clear plan for how you will move around the classroom during different activities. Identify areas where you need to focus based on student needs, such as group work or independent tasks.
- **Target Specific Groups**: Rotate your attention among different groups or individual students to ensure that everyone receives feedback and support throughout the lesson.

Use of Proximity

- **Close Proximity**: Position yourself near students who may need extra support or encouragement. Your physical presence can deter off-task behavior and provide a sense of security for those struggling with the material.
- **Positive Reinforcement**: Use proximity to offer praise and encouragement. Standing near engaged students allows you to provide immediate positive feedback, reinforcing their efforts.

Engaging Questions

- **Ask Open-Ended Questions**: Encourage deeper thinking and discussion by asking open-ended questions as you circulate. This invites students to elaborate on their ideas and promotes critical thinking.
- **Check for Understanding**: Use questions to gauge comprehension. For example, ask students to explain their reasoning or summarize what they have learned, allowing you to assess their understanding.

Interactive Feedback

- **Provide Immediate Feedback**: As you move around, offer timely feedback on students' work. This could be in the form of verbal comments or quick suggestions for improvement, helping students adjust their approach in real time.
- **Use Student Names**: Personalize your interactions by using students' names when providing feedback. This fosters a sense of belonging and shows that you are attentive to their contributions.

Utilize Technology

- **Digital Check-Ins**: If appropriate, use technology tools like polls or apps to check in with students while you circulate. This can facilitate quick feedback and gauge student engagement.
- **Collaborative Platforms**: Encourage students to share their progress on digital platforms, allowing you to monitor their work and provide feedback as you circulate.

Encourage Peer Interaction

- **Facilitate Peer Discussions**: As you circulate, encourage students to discuss their work with peers. This not only fosters collaboration but also allows you to assess their understanding in a group context.
- **Group Roles**: Assign specific roles within groups (e.g., note-taker, presenter) to encourage accountability and ensure that all students are actively participating in discussions.

Checklists and Tracking

- **Use Checklists**: Create checklists for students to track their progress during independent work. Circulate to help them stay on task and address any questions or concerns.
- **Progress Monitoring**: Develop a system for tracking student engagement and participation as you circulate. This could involve quick notes or digital tracking to identify who may need additional support.

Scheduled Circulation Time

- **Designate Circulation Time**: Set specific times during the lesson when you will circulate. Communicate this to students so they know when to expect your attention and support.
- **Mix It Up**: Vary your circulation routine to keep students engaged and to ensure that you are observing different areas of the classroom.

Nonverbal Communication

- **Use Body Language**: Employ nonverbal cues, such as nodding or thumbs up, to show encouragement and support as you circulate. Positive body language can enhance student confidence.
- **Facial Expressions**: Smile and maintain an approachable demeanor to create a welcoming atmosphere that encourages student engagement.

Reflective Practice

- **Self-Reflection**: After lessons, reflect on your circulation and engagement strategies. Consider what worked well and what could be improved for future classes.
- **Solicit Feedback**: Ask students for feedback on how your circulation and engagement practices affect their learning experience. This can help you refine your approach.

Circulating the classroom and engaging with students are essential practices for effective teaching. **By employing strategies such as purposeful movement, engaging questions, interactive feedback, and encouraging peer interaction, teachers can foster a supportive and dynamic learning environment. These strategies not only enhance student understanding and participation but also build stronger relationships,** ultimately contributing to a more positive classroom culture. Through thoughtful circulation and engagement, educators can create an atmosphere where all students feel valued and empowered to succeed.

"Techniques for Observing Behavior without Being Intrusive"

Observing student behavior effectively while maintaining a non-intrusive presence is crucial for creating a positive learning environment. Teachers need to gather insights into student interactions, engagement, and understanding without disrupting the flow of learning. Here are several techniques to achieve this balance:

Active Listening

- **Engage with the Environment**: Position yourself in a way that allows you to hear conversations without interrupting them. This can involve standing to the side or slightly behind groups of students.
- **Observe Nonverbal Cues**: Pay attention to body language, facial expressions, and gestures. These nonverbal signals can provide valuable information about student engagement and interactions.

Strategic Seating

- **Move around the Classroom**: Circulate the room casually. **By positioning yourself among students rather than at the front**, you can observe their behavior more naturally without drawing attention to your observations.
- **Utilize Flexible Seating**: If possible, use flexible seating arrangements that allow you to observe from different angles, making it easier to see interactions without being overly intrusive.

Anecdotal Records

- **Take Notes Discreetly**: Use a small notebook or digital device to jot down observations without interrupting the lesson. This helps you remember specific behaviors or interactions for later reflection.
- **Focus on Patterns**: Look for trends or patterns in behavior over time rather than fixating on isolated incidents. This long-term perspective allows for a more comprehensive understanding of student dynamics.

Nonverbal Monitoring

- **Use Subtle Signals**: Develop a system of nonverbal signals or cues that can communicate expectations without interrupting the lesson. For example, a gentle nod or thumbs-up can provide encouragement without breaking focus.
- **Facial Expressions**: Maintain an approachable and open demeanor. Smiling or nodding can encourage students to engage without feeling scrutinized.

Designated Observation Areas

- **Create Observation Zones**: Set up areas in the classroom where you can observe without being in the middle of the action. This could be a corner of the room or a designated seating area where you can monitor student behavior more discreetly.
- **Use Mirrors**: If feasible, place mirrors in the classroom to allow for indirect observation of student interactions without being physically present in the space.

Engaging Through Activities

- **Participate in Group Work**: Join students during group activities as a participant rather than an observer. This allows you to gather insights while contributing to the task, creating a less intrusive observation experience.
- **Rotate Roles**: Encourage students to take turns leading activities or discussions. By stepping back, you can observe their leadership and collaboration without actively directing the flow.

Peer Observations

- **Involve Colleagues**: Invite fellow teachers to observe your classroom. They can provide an external perspective on student behavior and classroom dynamics without you having to be the sole observer.

- **Student Feedback**: Use informal surveys or check-ins to gather student feedback about classroom interactions and dynamics. This can provide insights without requiring direct observation.

Structured Observation Frameworks

- **Use Checklists or Rubrics**: Develop simple checklists or rubrics that outline specific behaviors you want to observe. This structured approach allows for focused observations without feeling intrusive.

- **Focus on Specific Goals**: Identify key behaviors or interactions to observe during a lesson. Having a specific focus helps you gather data without feeling overwhelmed or intrusive.

Reflection and Debriefing

- **Post-Activity Reflection**: After activities, take a few minutes to reflect on observed behaviors. Encourage students to share their thoughts on the group dynamics, allowing for insight without direct observation during the activity.

- **Class Discussions**: Hold regular class discussions about collaboration and interaction. This opens a dialogue about behavior and engagement, providing insights into student perspectives without direct observation.

Observing student behavior without being intrusive is essential for maintaining a positive learning environment and gathering valuable insights. **By employing techniques such as active listening, strategic seating, discreet note-taking, and engaging through activities, teachers can effectively monitor student dynamics while minimizing disruption. These practices foster a sense of trust and openness, encouraging students to engage more freely and enhancing the overall classroom experience.** Through thoughtful observation, educators can support student growth and learning while respecting their space and autonomy.

"Using Data to Inform Classroom Management"

Effective classroom management is essential for creating an optimal learning environment. One of the most powerful tools educators can utilize is data. By systematically collecting and analyzing data on student behavior, engagement, and academic performance, teachers can make informed decisions that enhance classroom management strategies. This essay explores how data can be used to inform classroom management practices, the types of data that can be collected, and the benefits of a data-driven approach.

Types of Data to Collect

Behavioral Data

- **Incident Reports**: Record instances of disruptive behavior, including frequency, duration, and context. This helps identify patterns and triggers.
- **Behavior Checklists**: Use checklists to monitor specific behaviors (e.g., on-task behavior, participation) throughout lessons.

Academic Performance Data

- **Assessments**: Analyze scores from quizzes, tests, and assignments to identify areas where students are struggling or excelling.
- **Classwork and Homework**: Monitor completion rates and quality of assignments to gauge student engagement and understanding.

Attendance and Participation Data

- **Attendance Records**: Track student attendance and tardiness, as these can correlate with engagement and behavior issues.
- **Participation Logs**: Keep track of student participation in class discussions and activities to identify disengaged students.

Survey and Feedback Data

- **Student Surveys**: Conduct surveys to gather student feedback on classroom climate, teaching effectiveness, and areas for improvement.
- **Peer Observations**: Use feedback from colleagues who observe your classroom to gain insights into management strategies and student interactions.

Analyzing Data

1. **Identifying Trends and Patterns**
   - Analyze the data to identify trends over time. For example, look for patterns in behavioral incidents related to specific times of day, types of activities, or particular students.
   - Use graphs and charts to visualize data trends, making it easier to identify correlations between behavior and academic performance.
2. **Setting Goals**
   - Based on data analysis, set specific, measurable goals for classroom management. For example, if data shows high levels of disruption during group work, a goal might be to reduce incidents by a certain percentage.
3. **Adjusting Strategies**
   - Use data to inform decisions about instructional practices and management strategies. If certain activities correlate with higher engagement, consider incorporating more of those types of activities.
   - Adjust seating arrangements or group compositions based on behavioral data to promote positive interactions.

Implementing Data-Driven Strategies

Targeted Interventions

- Develop targeted interventions for students exhibiting challenging behaviors based on data analysis. For example, if a student frequently disrupts class during specific activities, implement a personalized behavior plan.
- Use academic data to provide differentiated instruction tailored to students' needs, ensuring all students can engage successfully.

Communication with Stakeholders

- Share relevant data with students and parents to foster transparency and collaboration. For instance, discussing attendance and participation data can help students take ownership of their learning.
- Engage with school administrators and support staff using data to advocate for additional resources or interventions needed in the classroom.

Ongoing Monitoring and Reflection

- Continuously collect and analyze data to assess the effectiveness of implemented strategies. This allows for ongoing refinement and adjustment based on what works best for your students.
- Reflect on data outcomes in collaboration with colleagues to share successful practices and learn from each other's experiences.

Benefits of a Data-Driven Approach

Informed Decision-Making

- Data-driven management allows teachers to make informed decisions based on evidence rather than intuition. This leads to more effective and targeted classroom strategies.

Increased Accountability

- By utilizing data, educators can hold themselves accountable for student outcomes and demonstrate the impact of their management strategies on student success.

Enhanced Student Support

- A data-driven approach enables more tailored support for individual students, promoting a more inclusive and responsive classroom environment.

Improved Classroom Climate

- Understanding student behaviors and academic needs through data can help create a more positive classroom climate, leading to increased student engagement and satisfaction.

Using data to inform classroom management is a powerful strategy that enhances teaching effectiveness and student success. **By systematically collecting and analyzing behavioral, academic, attendance, and feedback data, educators can make informed decisions that improve classroom dynamics and support student learning. This data-driven approach not only promotes accountability and tailored interventions but also fosters a more positive and engaging learning environment for all students.** Ultimately, by leveraging data effectively, teachers can create classrooms that support growth, engagement, and success for every learner.

"Collecting Data on Student Behavior and Performance"

Collecting data on student behavior and performance is essential for effective classroom management and instructional improvement. By systematically gathering and analyzing this data, educators can make informed decisions that enhance student learning outcomes and create a positive classroom environment. This essay explores the types of data that can be collected, methods for gathering this data, and the importance of a structured approach to data collection.

Types of Data to Collect

Behavioral Data

- **Incident Reports**: Document occurrences of disruptive behavior, including details about what happened, when, and the context. This helps identify patterns and triggers.
- **Behavior Checklists**: Use checklists to monitor specific behaviors, such as on-task behavior, cooperation with peers, and adherence to classroom rules.

Academic Performance Data

- **Formative Assessments**: Gather data from quizzes, tests, and assignments to measure student understanding and progress. These assessments can provide insights into areas of strength and weakness.
- **Summative Assessments**: Analyze performance on larger assessments at the end of units or terms to evaluate overall learning and retention.

Engagement and Participation Data

- **Participation Logs**: Track student participation in discussions, group work, and class activities. This helps identify students who may be disengaged.

- **Attendance Records**: Monitor attendance and punctuality, as these factors can significantly impact student performance and classroom dynamics.

Feedback and Reflection Data

- **Student Surveys**: Conduct surveys to gather student feedback on their learning experiences, classroom climate, and perceived challenges.
- **Self-Assessment Tools**: Encourage students to reflect on their learning and behavior through self-assessment forms, allowing them to identify areas for improvement.

Methods for Collecting Data

Direct Observation

- **Informal Observations**: Teachers can observe student behavior during class activities, taking notes on interactions, engagement, and adherence to rules.
- **Structured Observations**: Use a structured observation tool or rubric to systematically assess specific behaviors or interactions during lessons.

Checklists and Rating Scales

- **Behavior Checklists**: Develop checklists that outline specific behaviors to observe during different activities, making it easier to track student behavior consistently.
- **Rating Scales**: Use rating scales to evaluate student engagement and participation, providing a quantitative measure of behaviors.

Digital Tools

- **Classroom Management Software**: Utilize digital tools and apps designed for tracking behavior and academic performance, allowing for real-time data collection and analysis.

- **Online Surveys**: Use online platforms to administer student surveys quickly and efficiently, collecting responses in an easily analyzable format.

Assessment Data

- **Quizzes and Tests**: Regularly administer quizzes and tests to gather data on student understanding and progress. Analyze results to identify trends and areas needing attention.
- **Assignment Tracking**: Monitor the completion and quality of assignments to assess student engagement and academic performance.

Peer Feedback

- **Collaborative Assessments**: Encourage students to provide feedback to each other on group projects or presentations, which can be compiled to assess collaborative skills and engagement.
- **Peer Observations**: Involve colleagues in observing your classroom, gathering their feedback on student behavior and interactions to provide an external perspective.

Importance of Structured Data Collection

Consistency and Reliability

- A structured approach to data collection ensures consistency across observations and assessments, making the data more reliable and valid for analysis.
- Clear guidelines for data collection help minimize bias and increase the accuracy of the information gathered.

Informed Decision-Making

- Collecting comprehensive data enables educators to make informed decisions about instructional strategies and classroom management practices based on evidence rather than intuition.

- By analyzing trends and patterns, teachers can identify which strategies are effective and which need adjustment.

Targeted Interventions

- Data collection allows for the identification of students who may need additional support, enabling targeted interventions tailored to their specific needs.
- Early identification of behavioral or academic challenges can lead to timely interventions, helping to prevent issues from escalating.

Continuous Improvement

- Regular data collection fosters a culture of continuous improvement, encouraging educators to reflect on their practices and make adjustments as necessary.
- Ongoing analysis of data helps track student progress over time, allowing for adjustments in teaching methods to enhance learning outcomes.

Collecting data on student behavior and performance is crucial for effective classroom management and instructional improvement. By utilizing various methods such as direct observation, checklists, digital tools, and assessments, educators can gather valuable insights into student engagement and understanding. A structured approach to data collection enhances consistency, informs decision-making, enables targeted interventions, and promotes continuous improvement. Ultimately, leveraging data effectively empowers educators to create a positive and productive learning environment that supports all students in achieving their full potential.

"Great teachers build lasting connections with their students, transforming the classroom into a safe space for growth, curiosity, and mutual respect."

"Adjusting Management Strategies Based on Observation and Feedback"

Effective classroom management is a dynamic process that requires constant reflection and adaptation. Educators must be willing to adjust their management strategies based on observations of student behavior and feedback from various sources. This flexibility is essential for creating a responsive learning environment that meets the diverse needs of students.

Importance of Adjusting Management Strategies

Responsive Teaching

- Adapting management strategies based on observations allows educators to respond to the unique dynamics of their classrooms. This responsiveness helps address issues before they escalate, ensuring a more positive learning environment.

Meeting Diverse Needs

- Students have varying needs, learning styles, and behavioral tendencies. Regularly assessing and adjusting management strategies helps teachers tailor their approaches to support all learners effectively.

Improving Student Engagement

- By observing student behavior and collecting feedback, educators can identify factors that contribute to disengagement. Adjusting strategies to address these factors can enhance student motivation and participation.

Enhancing Classroom Climate

- A flexible management approach fosters a supportive classroom atmosphere. When students see that their needs and feedback are considered, it builds trust and a sense of community.

Methods for Gathering Observation and Feedback

Direct Observation

- Regularly observe student interactions, engagement, and behavior during various activities. Take notes on specific behaviors, participation levels, and group dynamics to identify patterns.

Student Feedback

- Conduct surveys or informal check-ins to gather student perspectives on classroom management, teaching methods, and areas for improvement. Encourage honest feedback to inform your practices.

Peer Observations

- Invite colleagues to observe your classroom and provide feedback on management strategies. They can offer valuable insights from an outside perspective, highlighting areas for growth.

Reflective Practice

- Engage in self-reflection after lessons to assess the effectiveness of your management strategies. Consider what worked well and what could be improved based on your observations.

Behavioral Data Analysis

- Analyze data on student behavior, participation, and academic performance. Look for trends and correlations that may indicate the need for adjustments in management approaches.

Practical Approaches to Implementing Changes

Set Specific Goals

- Based on observations and feedback, identify specific areas for improvement in your management strategies. Setting clear, achievable goals will help guide your adjustments and track progress.

Try New Strategies

- Experiment with different management techniques that align with your observations. For example, if students struggle with group work, consider implementing structured roles or clearer expectations to facilitate collaboration.

Adjust Routines and Procedures

- Reevaluate classroom routines and procedures based on student feedback. Streamlining transitions or modifying expectations can enhance overall classroom management and student engagement.

Communicate Changes

- Clearly communicate any adjustments to your management strategies with students. Explain the rationale behind the changes and how they will benefit the learning environment. This transparency fosters buy-in from students.

Monitor and Reflect

- After implementing adjustments, continue to observe student behavior and gather feedback to assess the effectiveness of the changes. Regular reflection will help you determine if further modifications are needed.

Professional Development

- Engage in professional development opportunities focused on classroom management. Learning new strategies and techniques can provide fresh perspectives and resources for adjusting your approach.

Adjusting management strategies based on observation and feedback is essential for creating an effective and responsive classroom environment. **By employing methods such as direct observation, student feedback, and data analysis, educators can identify areas for improvement and implement targeted changes. This flexibility not only enhances student engagement and supports diverse learning needs but also fosters a positive classroom climate**. Ultimately, the willingness to adapt and refine management strategies is a hallmark of effective teaching, leading to improved outcomes for all students.

Chapter 7

Addressing Disruptive Behavior in the Classroom

> ***"The dream begins, most of the time, with a teacher who believes in you, who tugs and pushes and leads you on to the next plateau, sometimes poking you with a sharp stick called truth."***
>
> *— Dan Rather*

Disruptive behavior in the classroom can significantly hinder the learning process, affecting not only the individual student involved but also their peers and the overall classroom environment. Effective classroom management is crucial in addressing and mitigating disruptive behaviors. This essay explores the causes of disruptive behavior, strategies for prevention and intervention, and the importance of fostering a positive classroom climate.

Understanding Disruptive Behavior

Causes of Disruptive Behavior

- **Individual Factors**: Some students may exhibit disruptive behavior due to underlying issues such as learning difficulties, emotional challenges, or unmet needs.

- **Environmental Factors**: Classroom dynamics, including group interactions, teaching methods, and classroom layout, can contribute to disruptions.
- **Social Influences**: Peer pressure and the desire for social acceptance can lead students to act out, especially in group settings.

Impact of Disruptive Behavior

- Disruptive behavior can interrupt instruction, distract other students, and create a chaotic classroom atmosphere. It can also lead to increased stress for teachers and affect overall student achievement.

Strategies for Addressing Disruptive Behavior

Preventive Measures

- **Establish Clear Expectations**: Set clear rules and expectations for behavior from the outset. Communicate these expectations regularly and involve students in the rule-making process.
- **Create a Positive Classroom Environment**: Foster a welcoming and inclusive atmosphere that encourages respect and collaboration. Use strategies such as cooperative learning and team-building activities.
- **Engage Students**: Design engaging and relevant lessons that capture students' interests. When students are actively engaged, they are less likely to exhibit disruptive behavior.

Proactive Monitoring

- **Circulate the Classroom**: Actively monitor student behavior by circulating the classroom during activities. Proximity can deter potential disruptions and allow for immediate intervention if needed.
- **Nonverbal Cues**: Use nonverbal signals, such as eye contact or gestures, to redirect students without interrupting the flow of the lesson.

Intervention Strategies

- **Immediate Redirection**: Address disruptive behavior promptly and privately, if possible. Use a calm and respectful tone to redirect the student's attention back to the task at hand.
- **Positive Reinforcement**: Recognize and reward positive behavior. Praise students who are following the rules, which can motivate others to do the same.
- **Restorative Practices**: When addressing serious disruptions, consider restorative approaches that focus on repairing harm and restoring relationships. This can involve discussions with the student to understand their behavior and work toward solutions.

Structured Consequences

- **Implement Consequences**: Clearly outline the consequences for disruptive behavior. Ensure that consequences are fair, consistent, and proportional to the behavior exhibited.
- **Reflection and Accountability**: Encourage students to reflect on their behavior and understand its impact on others. This can involve writing a reflection or participating in a restorative circle.

Individualized Support

- **Identify Underlying Issues**: For persistent disruptive behavior, assess whether there are underlying issues affecting the student. This may involve discussions with the student, parents, or school counselors.
- **Develop Behavior Plans**: Create individualized behavior plans for students who require additional support. These plans should outline specific goals, strategies, and supports tailored to the student's needs.

Fostering a Positive Classroom Climate

Build Strong Relationships

- Establish trust and rapport with students by showing genuine interest in their lives and well-being. Strong relationships can lead to increased respect and reduced disruptive behavior.

Encourage Student Voice

- Involve students in decision-making processes related to classroom rules and activities. Empowering students to contribute fosters a sense of ownership and responsibility.

Provide Emotional Support

- Create a safe space for students to express their feelings and concerns. Incorporate social-emotional learning practices to help students develop self-regulation and interpersonal skills.

Promote Inclusivity

- Ensure that all students feel valued and included. Recognize and celebrate diversity within the classroom, which can enhance community and reduce the likelihood of disruptive behavior.

Addressing disruptive behavior in the classroom requires a multifaceted approach that includes prevention, proactive monitoring, effective interventions, and fostering a positive climate. By understanding the underlying causes of disruptive behavior and implementing targeted strategies, educators can create an environment conducive to learning and growth. Ultimately, a focus on building relationships, promoting inclusivity, and engaging students will lead to a more harmonious classroom where all students can thrive.

"Preventive Strategies for Addressing Disruptive Behavior in the Classroom"

Preventive strategies are essential for fostering a positive classroom environment and minimizing disruptive behavior before it occurs. **By proactively addressing potential issues, educators can create a supportive atmosphere** that promotes learning and engagement.

Establish Clear Expectations

- **Develop Rules Together**: Involve students in creating classroom rules to foster a sense of ownership and accountability. When students contribute to the rule-making process, they are more likely to understand and adhere to the expectations.
- **Communicate Expectations**: Clearly **articulate rules and procedures at the beginning of the school year and revisit them regularly**. Use visual aids, such as posters or charts, to reinforce expectations in the classroom.

Create a Positive Classroom Environment

- **Foster Inclusivity**: Cultivate a classroom culture that **values diversity and inclusivity**. Encourage students to **respect each other's differences and create a sense of belonging.**
- **Establish Routines**: Implement consistent daily routines that provide structure and predictability. Routines help students know what to expect, reducing anxiety and potential disruptions.

Engage Students Actively

- **Interactive Lessons**: Design lessons that involve active participation, such as group discussions, hands-on activities, and collaborative projects. Engaged students are less likely to become disruptive.
- **Differentiated Instruction**: Tailor instruction to meet the diverse needs of students. By providing varied learning opportunities, you can keep students motivated and focused.

Build Strong Relationships

- **Get to Know Your Students**: Take the time to learn about **your students' interests, strengths, and challenges.** Building rapport fosters trust and respect, making students more likely to engage positively in the classroom.

- **Regular Check-Ins**: Conduct **informal check-ins with students to gauge their emotional well-being and academic progress**. This proactive approach can help identify potential issues early on.

Use Proactive Monitoring

- **Circulate the Classroom**: Move around the classroom during activities to monitor student behavior. Proximity can deter disruptions and allow for timely interventions.

- **Nonverbal Signals**: Use subtle nonverbal cues, such as eye contact or gestures, to redirect students without interrupting the flow of the lesson.

Implement Social-Emotional Learning (SEL)

- **Teach Self-Regulation Skills**: Incorporate SEL practices that help students **develop self-awareness, self-management, and interpersonal skills.** Teaching students how to manage their emotions can reduce disruptive behavior.

- **Conflict Resolution Training**: Provide students with tools and strategies for resolving conflicts peacefully. This equips them to handle disagreements constructively and reduces the likelihood of disruptions.

Create a Safe and Supportive Environment

- **Encourage Open Communication**: Foster an environment where students feel comfortable expressing their thoughts and feelings. Encourage them to voice concerns without fear of judgment.

- **Provide Emotional Support**: Be attentive to students' emotional needs and offer support when necessary. **A caring teacher can make a significant difference** in a student's willingness to engage appropriately.

Involve Families and Caregivers

- **Communicate with Parents**: Establish regular communication with parents and caregivers about classroom expectations and student behavior. Involving families can reinforce positive behavior at home.
- **Collaborative Goal-Setting**: Work with families to set behavior goals for students. Collaborative approaches create a unified support system for the student.

Reflect and Adjust

- **Regular Self-Reflection**: Engage in **self-reflection to assess your teaching practices and classroom management strategies**. Consider what is working well and what might need adjustment.
- **Solicit Feedback**: Encourage feedback from students about the classroom environment and management strategies. Their insights can help you make informed adjustments.

Implementing preventive strategies is crucial for minimizing disruptive behavior and creating a learning environment. **By establishing clear expectations, fostering strong relationships, engaging students actively, and creating a safe and supportive classroom, educators can significantly reduce disruptions. These proactive measures not only enhance classroom management but also promote student well-being and academic success.** Ultimately, a focus on prevention sets the foundation for a positive and productive learning experience for all students.

"Techniques for Identifying and Addressing Potential Disruptions Before They Escalate"

Preventing classroom disruptions requires **vigilance and proactive strategies that help educators identify and address issues before they escalate**. By implementing effective techniques, teachers can maintain a positive learning environment. Here are key strategies for recognizing and managing potential disruptions early on.

Observational Techniques

- **Regular Monitoring**: Consistently observe student behavior during lessons. **Look for signs of disengagement, restlessness, or negative interactions among peers.** Early identification can help address issues promptly.
- **Behavioral Checklists**: Utilize **checklists to track specific behaviors that might indicate potential disruptions, such as off-task behavior or frequent talking out of turn.** This systematic approach helps identify patterns over time.

Understanding Student Needs

- **Know Your Students**: Build strong relationships with students to understand their **individual needs, interests, and triggers for disruptive behavior.** This knowledge can help anticipate challenges.
- **Emotional Check-Ins**: Conduct regular emotional check-ins through **informal conversations or quick surveys**. This can provide insights into students' moods and help identify those who may be feeling overwhelmed.

Setting Clear Expectations

- **Define Classroom Norms**: Clearly **communicate rules and expectations at the start of the year** and reinforce them regularly. Involving students in this process can enhance their sense of ownership.
- **Visual Reminders**: Use posters or charts displaying classroom expectations to serve as constant reminders for students, helping to reinforce positive behavior.

Engaging Instructional Practices

- **Active Learning**: Incorporate interactive activities that encourage participation, such as **group work and hands-on tasks.** Engaged students are less likely to disrupt the learning process.

- **Variety in Teaching Methods**: Employ **diverse teaching strategies to cater to different learning styles. Keeping lessons dynamic and interesting can maintain student focus.**

Proactive Classroom Management

- **Strategic Seating Arrangements**: Organize seating to minimize potential distractions or conflicts. Placing students who may struggle with behavior in easily observable locations can enhance monitoring.

- **Routine Transitions**: Establish clear procedures for transitioning between activities. Practicing these routines helps reduce downtime and keeps students focused.

Communication Techniques

- **Nonverbal Signals**: Develop nonverbal cues (such as hand signals) to communicate with students when they need to adjust their behavior without interrupting the lesson.

- **Positive Reinforcement**: Acknowledge and praise students for positive behavior. This encourages a culture of respect and cooperation, reducing the likelihood of disruptions.

Conflict Prevention Strategies

- **Teach Conflict Resolution**: Equip students with strategies for resolving conflicts constructively. **Role-playing scenarios** can provide valuable practice for handling disagreements.

- **Monitor Group Dynamics**: Pay close attention to interactions during group activities. If conflicts arise, intervene early to redirect focus and maintain a positive atmosphere.

Regular Reflection and Adjustment

- **Reflect on Lessons**: After each lesson, **evaluate what went well and what could be improved. Identify moments where potential disruptions** could have been addressed more effectively.
- **Solicit Student Feedback**: Encourage students to share their perspectives on classroom dynamics. Their input can offer insights into potential issues and inform future strategies.

Identifying and addressing potential disruptions before they escalate is essential for maintaining an effective learning environment. **By employing observational techniques, understanding student needs, setting clear expectations, and using proactive management strategies, educators can significantly reduce disruptions**. A focus on prevention not only fosters a positive classroom culture but also supports student engagement and academic success, laying the foundation for a productive educational experience.

"Creating a Culture of Respect and Responsibility in the Classroom"

Establishing a culture of respect and responsibility is crucial for fostering a positive learning environment where students **feel safe, valued, and empowered to succeed.** This culture enhances **student engagement, reduces disruptive behavior, and promotes collaboration**.

Set Clear Expectations

- **Define Respect and Responsibility**: Clearly articulate what respect and responsibility look like in the classroom. Discuss behaviors such as **listening, valuing diverse opinions, and taking ownership** of one's actions.
- **Collaborative Rule-Making**: Involve students in creating classroom rules. When students participate in the rule-making process, they are more likely to understand and commit to these expectations.

Model Respectful Behavior

- **Demonstrate Positive Interactions**: As the teacher, model respectful communication and behavior. **Use polite language, listen actively to students, and acknowledge their contributions**.
- **Share Personal Responsibility**: Share your **own experiences of responsibility and accountability**. This openness encourages students to take similar ownership of their actions.

Promote Open Communication

- **Encourage Dialogue**: Create opportunities for **students to express their thoughts and feelings in a safe environment**. Regularly check in with students to ensure they feel heard and respected.
- **Foster Active Listening**: Teach students the importance of listening to one another. Use activities that require active listening and respectful responses to promote these skills.

Implement Collaborative Learning

- **Group Activities**: Incorporate collaborative projects that **require teamwork and communication.** Working together fosters a sense of community and reinforces the values of respect and responsibility.
- **Peer Feedback**: Encourage students to **give and receive constructive feedback.** This practice helps them learn to respect differing opinions and perspectives.

Recognize and Reinforce Positive Behavior

- **Praise Respectful Actions**: Acknowledge and **reward students who demonstrate respect and responsibility.** Positive reinforcement encourages others to follow suit and reinforces desired behaviors.
- **Celebrate Achievements**: Celebrate both individual and collective achievements, creating a culture that values effort and success.

Create a Safe Environment

- **Encourage Inclusivity**: Ensure that all students **feel valued and included in classroom activities.** Address any forms of exclusion or discrimination promptly to maintain a respectful atmosphere.
- **Establish Trust**: Build strong **relationships with students based on trust**. When students feel safe, they are more likely to take responsibility for their actions and treat others with respect.

Teach Social-Emotional Skills

- **Integrate SEL Programs**: Incorporate **social-emotional learning (SEL)** into the curriculum. Teaching **skills like empathy, self-regulation, and conflict resolution can enhance students' abilities to interact respectfully**.
- **Role-Playing Scenarios**: Use role-playing activities to help students practice respectful communication and responsible decision-making in various situations.

Reflect on Behavior and Consequences

- **Teach Accountability**: When students make mistakes, **guide them through the process of reflecting on their behavior and understanding its impact on others.** Encourage them to take responsibility for their actions.

- **Restorative Practices**: Implement restorative approaches that focus on repairing harm and rebuilding relationships. This emphasizes accountability while fostering a culture of respect.

Creating a culture of respect and responsibility in the classroom is fundamental for fostering a positive learning environment. **By setting clear expectations, modeling respectful behavior, promoting open communication, and implementing collaborative learning, educators can cultivate an atmosphere where students feel valued and empowered. Recognizing positive behavior and teaching social-emotional skills further strengthens this culture.** Ultimately, a respectful and responsible classroom not only enhances student engagement but also prepares students for success both academically and socially.

"Responding to Misbehavior in the Classroom"

Addressing misbehavior effectively is crucial for maintaining a positive learning environment and fostering student growth. The way educators respond to misbehavior can influence student behavior, emotional well-being, and the overall classroom atmosphere.

Stay Calm and Collected

- **Maintain Composure**: When misbehavior occurs, it's essential to remain calm. A composed response sets a positive tone and helps de-escalate the situation.
- **Avoid Emotional Reactions**: Responding **with frustration or anger can escalate the situation.** Take a moment to breathe and gather your thoughts before addressing the behavior.

Address the Behavior, Not the Student

- **Focus on Actions**: Clearly differentiate between the student and their behavior. **Use language that addresses the specific behavior** (e.g., "Talking during instruction is disruptive") rather than labeling the student (e.g., "You are being bad").
- **Encourage Reflection**: Prompt the **student to reflect on their actions.** Ask questions like, "What happened?" and "How do you think it affected others?" to encourage accountability.

Use Nonverbal Cues

- **Establish Signals**: Utilize nonverbal cues **(like eye contact or a gesture) to redirect students discreetly.** This can help maintain the flow of the lesson while addressing the behavior.
- **Proximity Control**: Move **closer to the student displaying misbehavior.** Often, just your presence can be a powerful reminder to refocus.

Implement a Range of Responses

- **Verbal Warnings**: Start with a **verbal reminder of expectations**. This can often be enough to redirect behavior without further intervention.
- **Time-Outs or Cool-Downs**: If misbehavior persists, **provide the student with a brief time-out to reflect.** This can help them regain self-control before rejoining the class.
- **Loss of Privileges**: For repeated or severe misbehavior, consider implementing consequences, such as **loss of privileges (e.g., participation in a fun activity)**. Ensure that consequences are related to the behavior.

Encourage Problem-Solving

- **Involve the Student**: After addressing the misbehavior, **involve the student in discussing potential solutions**. Ask, "What could you do differently next time?" This empowers them to take responsibility for their actions.
- **Collaborative Solutions**: Encourage students to brainstorm strategies for avoiding similar behaviors in the future. This promotes critical thinking and accountability.

Reinforce Positive Behavior

- **Recognize Improvement**: Acknowledge and **praise students when they demonstrate positive behavior after misbehavior**. This reinforcement can encourage a shift toward more appropriate actions.
- **Create a Positive Environment**: Foster a classroom culture that values and celebrates respectful behavior. Highlighting good behavior among peers can motivate others to follow suit.

Communicate with Parents or Guardians

- **Keep Lines Open**: Maintain **open communication with parents regarding their child's behavior**. Share both positive and negative instances to provide a balanced view.
- **Collaborative Approach**: Work with parents to **create a consistent approach to behavior management**. This partnership can help reinforce expectations both at school and at home.

Reflect on Misbehavior Patterns

- **Identify Triggers**: Observe whether certain behaviors are recurring and try to identify underlying triggers. This can provide insights into patterns that need addressing.
- **Adjust Strategies**: If specific responses to misbehavior are not effective, be **willing to adjust your approach. Flexibility in your management strategies** can lead to better outcomes.

Responding to misbehavior in the classroom requires a balanced approach that emphasizes respect, accountability, and growth. **By staying calm, addressing behavior without labeling, and implementing a range of responses, educators can effectively manage misbehavior while promoting a positive learning environment. Encouraging student reflection, reinforcing positive behavior, and maintaining open communication with families' further support a culture of respect and responsibility.** Ultimately, effective responses to misbehavior not only mitigate disruptions but also contribute to the personal and social development of students.

"Strategies for Handling Disruptions Calmly and Effectively"

Managing disruptions in the classroom is an essential skill for educators. Handling these situations calmly and effectively can minimize interruptions and maintain a positive learning environment.

Stay Calm and Composed

- **Breathe and Pause**: Take a deep breath before responding to a disruption. A moment of pause can help you collect your thoughts and approach the situation more rationally.
- **Maintain a Neutral Tone**: Use a calm, steady voice when addressing the disruption. This conveys authority and reduces the chance of escalating tensions.

Set Clear Expectations

- **Establish Rules in Advance**: At the beginning of the year, communicate classroom rules and expectations clearly. Regularly revisit these expectations to reinforce them.
- **Use Visual Reminders**: Display rules prominently in the classroom. Visual aids serve as constant reminders and can help refocus students when disruptions occur.

Use Nonverbal Cues

- **Gestures and Eye Contact**: Employ subtle nonverbal cues, such as a gesture or direct eye contact, to signal to a student that they need to adjust their behavior. This approach can be less disruptive than verbal interventions.
- **Proximity Control**: Move closer to the student exhibiting disruptive behavior. Being nearby can serve as a reminder to refocus without interrupting the lesson.

Address the Disruption Immediately

- **Prompt Intervention**: Tackle disruptions promptly to prevent them from escalating. Address the behavior while it's happening, using a calm and firm approach.
- **Private Conversations**: If possible, address the disruptive behavior in a private conversation. This reduces embarrassment for the student and helps maintain a respectful environment.

Redirect Attention

- **Shift Focus**: Redirect the attention of the disruptive student or the entire class back to the lesson. Ask a question or introduce an engaging activity to recapture their interest.
- **Use Humor**: When appropriate, light humor can diffuse tension and redirect attention. However, be cautious not to undermine the seriousness of the situation.

Implement Structured Consequences

- **Consistent Consequences**: Clearly outline consequences for disruptive behavior and apply them consistently. This helps students understand the importance of following classroom rules.
- **Restorative Practices**: In cases of significant disruptions, consider restorative practices that focus on repairing harm and rebuilding relationships. This encourages accountability while promoting a supportive atmosphere.

Encourage Reflection

- **Prompt Self-Assessment**: After addressing the disruption, encourage the student to reflect on their behavior. Ask questions like, “How did your actions affect the class?” to promote self-awareness.

- **Problem-Solving Discussions**: Work with the student to brainstorm strategies for avoiding similar disruptions in the future. This empowers them to take responsibility for their actions.

Maintain Open Communication

- **Check-In with Students**: Regularly check in with students, both individually and as a group. This fosters a supportive environment and can help identify potential issues before they escalate.

- **Engage Parents**: Keep parents informed about their child's behavior and work collaboratively to address any recurring issues. A united approach can reinforce positive behavior both at school and at home.

Reflect on Classroom Management

- **Self-Reflection**: After a disruption, take time to reflect on the situation. Consider what triggered the behavior and whether your response was effective. Adjust your strategies as needed.

- **Solicit Feedback**: Encourage students to share their thoughts on classroom management and any disruptive incidents. Their insights can help you improve your approach.

Handling disruptions calmly and effectively is vital for maintaining a positive classroom environment. **By staying composed, setting clear expectations, using nonverbal cues, and addressing disruptions promptly, educators can manage behavior while fostering a respectful atmosphere. Encouraging reflection, maintaining open communication, and engaging in self-reflection further enhance classroom management.** Ultimately, these strategies not only mitigate disruptions but also contribute to a supportive and productive learning experience for all students.

"Restorative Approaches vs. Punitive Measures in Classroom Management"

Classroom management strategies can greatly influence student behavior, learning, and the overall school climate. **Two prominent approaches are restorative practices and punitive measures**. Each has its implications for addressing misbehavior and fostering a positive educational environment. This essay explores the differences between these two approaches, their benefits, and their potential drawbacks.

Restorative Approaches: Restorative approaches focus on repairing harm and restoring relationships rather than merely punishing the offender. This method emphasizes understanding the impact of behavior on others and encourages accountability.

Key Features:

- **Emphasis on Relationships**: Restorative practices prioritize building and maintaining positive relationships within the classroom. They encourage communication and empathy among students.
- **Accountability through Reflection**: Students are guided to reflect on their actions, understand the consequences of their behavior, and take responsibility for making amends.
- **Inclusive Dialogue**: Restorative approaches often involve all parties affected by the misbehavior—both the offender and the victim—in discussions aimed at healing and resolution.
- **Community Building**: These practices foster a sense of community and belonging, promoting a supportive classroom atmosphere.

Benefits:

- **Improved Relationships**: Restorative practices can strengthen relationships among students and between students and teachers, fostering a collaborative environment.

- **Reduced Recidivism**: Research shows that restorative approaches can lead to a decrease in repeat offenses, as students learn from their mistakes and understand the impact of their actions.
- **Enhanced Social Skills**: Students develop critical social-emotional skills, such as empathy, conflict resolution, and effective communication.

Potential Drawbacks:

- **Time-Consuming**: Implementing restorative practices can take time and may require more resources for training and facilitation.
- **Resistance from Some Students**: Some students may initially resist engaging in restorative discussions, especially if they are unaccustomed to such practices.

Punitive Measures: Punitive measures focus on imposing penalties or consequences for misbehavior, often with the intention of deterring future offenses. This approach typically emphasizes discipline through punishment rather than understanding.

Key Features:

- **Immediate Consequences**: Punitive measures often involve immediate consequences for misbehavior, such as detention, suspension, or loss of privileges.
- **Focus on Behavior**: The primary focus is on the behavior itself rather than its impact on others, leading to a more individualistic view of discipline.
- **Deterrent Effect**: The underlying assumption is that punishment will deter future misbehavior, leading students to think twice before acting out.

Benefits:

- **Quick Resolution**: Punitive measures can quickly address disruptive behavior, providing immediate consequences that may deter other students from similar actions.

- **Clear Boundaries**: Establishing clear rules and consequences can provide structure and help students understand the limits of acceptable behavior.

Potential Drawbacks:

- **Negative School Climate**: Over-reliance on punitive measures can create a hostile environment, where students feel alienated or fearful rather than supported.
- **Limited Learning Opportunities**: Punitive approaches often do not promote reflection or understanding of the underlying issues leading to misbehavior, limiting opportunities for personal growth.
- **Disproportionate Impact**: Research indicates that punitive measures can disproportionately affect marginalized students, contributing to systemic inequalities in education.

Both restorative approaches and punitive measures have their place in classroom management, but they serve different purposes and have distinct impacts on student behavior and school climate. **Restorative practices focus on healing and relationship-building, fostering a supportive and collaborative environment**. In contrast, **punitive measures emphasize immediate consequences and deterrence, which can sometimes lead to a negative school climate and limited personal growth for students**.

Ultimately, a balanced approach that incorporates elements of both strategies may be the most effective. Educators can create a positive learning environment by promoting accountability through restorative practices while still maintaining clear boundaries and consequences for unacceptable behavior. This combination encourages personal responsibility, empathy, and a sense of community, which are essential for fostering a successful educational experience.

Chapter 8

Promoting Student Engagement

> ***"The mediocre teacher tells. The good teacher explains. The superior teacher demonstrates. The great teacher inspires."***
> *— William Arthur Ward*

Student engagement is crucial for effective learning and academic success. Engaged students are more likely to participate actively, retain information, and develop a love for learning.

Create a Welcoming Environment

- **Foster Inclusivity**: Ensure that all **students feel valued and included.** Use diverse teaching materials that reflect various cultures and perspectives to make all students feel represented.
- **Establish a Positive Atmosphere**: Cultivate a classroom environment **where mistakes are seen as learning opportunities.** Encourage a growth mindset by praising effort and resilience.

Incorporate Active Learning Techniques

- **Hands-On Activities**: Use interactive activities, such as group projects, experiments, or simulations, to engage students physically and mentally.
- **Collaborative Learning**: Encourage students to work together in pairs or small groups. Collaboration promotes discussion, idea exchange, and peer support.

Utilize Varied Instructional Methods

- **Differentiate Instruction**: Tailor lessons to meet the diverse needs of students. **Use a mix of visual, auditory, and kinesthetic teaching** methods to cater to different learning styles.
- **Integrate Technology**: Incorporate technology, such as **educational apps or online resources,** to make learning more engaging and interactive.

Connect Learning to Real-Life Contexts

- **Relate Lessons to Students' Lives**: Help students see the relevance of what they're learning by connecting concepts to their personal experiences or current events.
- **Invite Guest Speakers**: Bring in professionals from various fields to share their experiences and insights. This exposure can inspire students and provide practical applications for their learning.

Encourage Student Voice and Choice

- **Involve Students in Decision-Making**: Allow students to have a say in classroom activities, topics of study, or project formats. This ownership increases their investment in the learning process.
- **Choice Boards**: Create options for assignments or projects, enabling students to choose how they demonstrate their understanding of a topic.

Set Clear Goals and Expectations

- **Goal Setting**: Help students set personal and academic goals. Regularly revisit these goals to encourage self-reflection and motivation.
- **Transparent Expectations**: Clearly communicate the objectives for each lesson. When students understand what is expected, they are more likely to engage.

Use Formative Assessment and Feedback

- **Frequent Check-Ins**: Use formative assessments, such as quizzes or exit tickets, to gauge understanding and adjust instruction accordingly. This helps students stay on track and feel supported.
- **Timely Feedback**: Provide constructive and timely feedback on assignments. Positive reinforcement encourages students to stay engaged and improve.

Incorporate Gamification

- **Game-Based Learning**: Use **game elements in lessons, such as points, badges, or leaderboards, to motivate students** and make learning fun.
- **Educational Games**: Incorporate educational **games that align with the curriculum, promoting engagement through competition and collaboration**.

Build Relationships

- **Get to Know Your Students**: Take time to learn about students' interests, strengths, and challenges. Building rapport fosters trust and encourages participation.
- **Create a Supportive Community**: Encourage peer interactions and build a sense of community in the classroom. Activities that promote teamwork can strengthen relationships among students.

Promoting student engagement is vital for creating a dynamic and effective learning environment. **By fostering a welcoming atmosphere, incorporating active learning techniques, connecting lessons to real-life contexts, and encouraging student voice and choice, educators can significantly enhance engagement levels. Additionally, utilizing varied instructional methods, setting clear goals, providing timely feedback, gamifying learning, and building relationships all contribute to a more engaged classroom.** Ultimately, when students feel connected, supported, and motivated, they are more likely to thrive academically and develop a lifelong love for learning.

"Strategies for Enhancing Student Engagement in the Classroom"

Promoting student engagement is essential for fostering a productive learning environment. Engaged students are **more motivated, attentive, and invested in their education**.

Active Learning Techniques

- **Group Work**: Encourage collaborative projects and peer discussions. Working in groups allows students to share ideas, learn from each other, and feel more involved in the learning process.
- **Hands-On Activities**: Use experiments, simulations, or creative projects to make learning interactive. Hands-on activities can help students better understand concepts by applying them in practical situations.

Variety in Instructional Methods

- **Differentiated Instruction**: Tailor lessons to meet diverse learning needs. Use a mix of teaching methods, **including lectures, discussions, videos, and interactive media,** to engage all students.
- **Flipped Classroom**: Assign **instructional content for homework (like videos or readings)** and use class time for discussions, problem-solving, and collaborative work. This model encourages active participation during class.

Connect Learning to Real Life

- **Relevance**: Relate lessons to students' interests, experiences, and current events. When students see the real-world applications of what they're learning, they are more likely to engage.
- **Guest Speakers and Field Trips**: Invite professionals or organize trips related to the subject matter. This exposure helps students understand the practical implications of their studies.

Encourage Student Voice and Choice

- **Choice Boards**: Provide options for assignments or projects, allowing students to choose how they want to demonstrate their understanding. This empowers them and increases investment in their work.
- **Surveys and Feedback**: Regularly solicit student input on topics, activities, and classroom policies. Implementing their suggestions can boost their sense of ownership.

Incorporate Technology

- **Interactive Tools**: Use **apps, online platforms, and multimedia presentations to create interactive learning experiences**. Tools like Kahoot! or Google Classroom can make lessons more engaging.
- **Digital Collaborations**: Facilitate online discussions or collaborative projects using technology. This can engage students who may be more comfortable expressing themselves in digital formats.

Gamification of Learning

- **Game Elements**: Integrate points, badges, or leaderboards into lessons to motivate students. Gamification can turn learning into a fun, competitive activity.
- **Educational Games**: Use games that align with the curriculum to make learning enjoyable and engaging.

Establish Clear Goals and Expectations

- **Goal Setting**: Help students set personal and academic goals. Revisit these goals regularly to track progress and keep students focused and motivated.
- **Transparent Learning Objectives**: Clearly outline the objectives for each lesson. When students understand what they are expected to achieve, they are more likely to engage.

Foster a Supportive Classroom Environment

- **Build Relationships**: Get to know your students' interests and backgrounds. A strong teacher-student relationship fosters trust and encourages participation.
- **Encourage a Growth Mindset**: Create an environment where mistakes are viewed as opportunities for learning. This encourages students to take risks and engage more fully in their learning.

Use Formative Assessment

- **Regular Check-Ins**: Use quick assessments, such as polls or exit tickets, to gauge understanding and adjust instruction as needed. This shows students that their learning is being monitored and valued.
- **Timely Feedback**: Provide constructive feedback on assignments and class participation. Acknowledging students' efforts and progress encourages continued engagement.

Enhancing student engagement is key to creating an effective learning environment. **By employing a variety of strategies—such as active learning, differentiated instruction, real-life connections, student choice, technology integration, Gamification, clear goals, supportive relationships, and formative assessment—educators can significantly boost engagement leve**ls. When students feel motivated, valued, and connected to their learning, they are more likely to thrive academically and develop a lifelong love for learning.

"Techniques for Keeping Students Actively Involved in Lessons"

Maintaining student engagement during lessons is vital for effective teaching and learning.

Interactive Questioning

- **Socratic Questioning**: Use **open-ended questions that encourage critical thinking and discussion. Prompt students to explain their reasoning** and engage with their peers' responses.
- **Think-Pair-Share**: Have students think about a question individually, **discuss it with a partner, and then share their insights with the class.** This method promotes participation and collaboration.

Hands-On Activities

- **Experiments and Demonstrations**: Incorporate science experiments or demonstrations that require student participation. **Hands-on activities** can make learning more tangible and memorable.
- **Role-Playing and Simulations**: Use role-playing to explore concepts in **subjects like history or literature**. Simulations can help students understand complex ideas by experiencing them in a controlled environment.

Group Work and Collaboration

- **Jigsaw Method**: Divide **students into small groups and assign each group a different topic**. After researching, each group presents their findings, ensuring that all students learn from one another.
- **Collaborative Projects**: Assign group projects that require teamwork and shared responsibilities. This fosters communication and enhances learning through collaboration.

Incorporate Technology

- **Interactive Tools**: Use platforms like Kahoot, Quiz, or Google Classroom to create interactive quizzes and activities. These tools make learning fun and engaging.
- **Digital Collaborations**: Utilize collaborative tools like Google Docs or Padlet for group work, allowing students to contribute and share ideas in real time.

Real-Life Connections

- **Relate Content to Students' Lives**: Connect **lessons to students' interests, experiences, or current events**. Making learning relevant enhances engagement and retention.
- **Field Trips and Guest Speakers**: Organize field trips or invite guest speakers who can provide practical insights related to the lesson. Real-world connections make the content more compelling.

Incorporate Movement

- **Brain Breaks**: Integrate **short movement breaks during lessons to re-energize students.** Activities like stretching or quick games can help maintain focus.
- **Learning Stations**: Set up different stations around the classroom where students can rotate and engage in various activities related to the lesson. This keeps them moving and involved.

Utilize Visual and Multimedia Aids

- **Videos and Visuals**: Use **short videos, infographics, or slideshows** to complement your teaching. Visual aids can help illustrate complex concepts and keep students engaged.
- **Interactive Whiteboards**: Incorporate technology like smart boards to encourage student interaction during lessons, such as solving problems or drawing diagrams.

Gamification

- **Game-Based Learning**: Introduce game elements into lessons, such as points, badges, or competitions. This approach can make learning enjoyable and motivate students to participate.

- **Challenges and Quests**: Create **challenges related to the lesson content**, allowing students to work toward specific goals in a fun and competitive way.

Regular Feedback and Reflection

- **Immediate Feedback**: Provide timely feedback on student participation and understanding. Acknowledging their contributions encourages continued involvement.

- **Reflective Practices**: Ask students to reflect on their learning at the end of each lesson. This can be done through journaling or group discussions, reinforcing their engagement and understanding.

Keeping students actively involved in lessons is essential for effective learning. **By employing a variety of techniques—such as interactive questioning, hands-on activities, group collaboration, technology integration, real-life connections, movement, visual aids, gamification, and regular feedback—educators can create a dynamic classroom environment**. Engaged students are more likely to participate, retain information, and develop a lifelong love for learning.

"Incorporating Interactive and Hands-On Learning Activities"

Interactive and hands-on learning activities are powerful tools for enhancing student engagement and deepening understanding. These approaches encourage active participation, collaboration, and practical application of knowledge.

Experiments and Investigations

- **Science Experiments**: Conduct **simple experiments that allow students to observe scientific principles in action**. For example, using everyday materials to explore chemical reactions can make learning tangible and exciting.
- **Inquiry-Based Learning**: Encourage **students to pose questions and investigate them through research and experimentation**. This fosters curiosity and critical thinking.

Project-Based Learning (PBL)

- **Real-World Projects**: Assign **projects that tackle real-world problems or challenges relevant to students' lives. For instance, students could design solutions for environmental issues** in their community.
- **Cross-Disciplinary Projects**: Integrate subjects by having students create **projects that require knowledge from multiple disciplines, such as combining art and science** to create a model of a cell.

Role-Playing and Simulations

- **Role-Playing**: Create scenarios where students assume different roles (e.g., historical figures, professionals) to explore concepts. This helps them understand diverse perspectives and the complexities of social interactions.
- **Simulations**: Use simulations to replicate real-life situations, **such as a mock government session or a business negotiation**. This interactive approach enhances engagement and application of skills.

Learning Stations

- **Station Rotation**: Set up different stations around the classroom, each focusing on a specific activity related to the lesson. **Students rotate through the stations, engaging in various hands-on tasks that reinforce** learning.

- **Choice Stations**: Provide options at each station, allowing students to choose activities based on their interests and learning preferences.

Collaborative Group Work

- **Team Projects**: Organize students into small groups to work on a shared project, such as creating a presentation or a poster. Collaboration promotes communication skills and fosters a sense of community.

- **Peer Teaching**: Encourage **students to teach each other concepts they have mastered.** This reinforces their understanding and builds confidence.

Use of Technology

- **Interactive Apps**: Incorporate educational apps and online platforms that allow students to engage with content interactively. Tools like Nearpod or Seesaw enable interactive lessons and real-time feedback.

- **Virtual Reality (VR)**: Utilize VR technology to provide immersive learning experiences, such as exploring historical sites or conducting virtual science labs.

Art and Creativity

- **Creative Projects**: Integrate art into lessons by allowing students to express their understanding through creative mediums, such as drawing, painting, or building models.

- **Storytelling and Drama**: Use **storytelling and drama activities to bring literature or historical events to life**. Students can act out scenes or create their own narratives based on what they've learned.

Field Trips and Outdoor Learning

- **Hands-On Experiences**: Organize **field trips to museums, nature reserves, or local businesses where students can engage directly** with the material. These experiences provide context and enhance understanding.
- **Outdoor Learning Activities**: Incorporate outdoor learning, such as nature walks or gardening projects, to teach concepts in a natural setting.

Reflection and Feedback

- **Post-Activity Reflection**: After hands-on activities, encourage students to **reflect on their experiences.** Ask questions about what they learned, what surprised them, and how they can apply their knowledge.
- **Peer Feedback**: Facilitate opportunities for students to give and receive feedback on their work. This collaborative critique can enhance understanding and encourage improvement.

Incorporating interactive and hands-on learning activities in the classroom fosters engagement and enhances understanding. **By utilizing experiments, project-based learning, role-playing, learning stations, collaborative work, technology, creativity, field trips, and reflective practices, educators can create a dynamic learning environment.** These approaches not only make learning more enjoyable but also empower students to take an active role in their education, leading to deeper comprehension and retention of knowledge.

"Encouraging Student Participation in the Classroom"

Encouraging student participation is vital for creating an engaging and effective learning environment. When students actively participate, they are more likely to understand and retain information.

Foster a Positive Classroom Atmosphere

- **Build Trust**: Create a safe space where students feel comfortable expressing their thoughts and opinions. Encourage respect and active listening among peers.
- **Celebrate Contributions**: Acknowledge all contributions, whether they are correct or incorrect. Positive reinforcement boosts confidence and encourages further participation.

Use Interactive Teaching Methods

- **Think-Pair-Share**: Ask a question, **give students time to think individually, and then discuss their thoughts with a partner before sharing with the larger group**. This structured approach allows quieter students to engage in discussion.
- **Socratic Seminars**: Facilitate discussions based on **open-ended questions**. Encourage students to respond to each other rather than solely to the teacher, fostering deeper dialogue.

Incorporate Technology

- **Polling and Quizzes**: Use tools like Poll Everywhere or Kahoot! to conduct live polls and quizzes. This interactive element can stimulate interest and encourage participation.
- **Discussion Forums**: Create online platforms where students can discuss topics outside of class. This allows students who may be hesitant to speak up in person to share their thoughts.

Implement Group Work

- **Collaborative Projects**: Assign group tasks that require cooperation and contribution from all members. Clearly define roles to ensure each student has a part to play.
- **Peer Teaching**: Encourage students to teach each other. This not only reinforces their understanding but also builds confidence and encourages active involvement.

Set Clear Expectations

- **Establish Norms**: Clearly communicate your expectations for participation and discussion. Establish classroom norms that promote respectful dialogue and encourage everyone to contribute.
- **Goal Setting**: Help students set individual participation goals. Reflecting on these goals regularly can motivate them to engage more actively.

Provide Choices

- **Choice in Activities**: Offer students options in how they participate or demonstrate understanding. This could include presentations, creative projects, or written reflections.
- **Interest-Based Topics**: Allow students to select topics that interest them for discussions or projects. When students are passionate about a subject, they are more likely to participate.

Use Engaging Content

- **Relatable Materials**: Incorporate materials that are relevant and relatable to students' lives. This connection can spark interest and encourage participation.
- **Multimedia Resources**: Use videos, podcasts, and interactive media to present content in varied ways, capturing student attention and encouraging involvement.

Encourage Questions

- **Question-Driven Learning**: Encourage **students to ask questions throughout the lesson**. Create a culture where curiosity is valued, and questions are seen as a vital part of the learning process.
- **Question Stems**: Provide **sentence starters or question stems to help students formulate their inquiries**. This can be particularly useful for students who may struggle to articulate their thoughts.

Incorporate Movement

- **Active Learning**: Include movement-based activities that require students to get up, move around, and engage with the content, such as scavenger hunts or gallery walks.
- **Interactive Stations**: Set up learning stations where students can rotate and participate in different activities. This keeps energy levels high and promotes involvement.

Encouraging student participation is essential for creating an engaging classroom environment. **By fostering a positive atmosphere, using interactive teaching methods, incorporating technology, implementing group work, setting clear expectations, providing choices, using engaging content, encouraging questions, and incorporating movement, educators can significantly enhance student involvement.** When students feel valued and empowered to participate, they are more likely to develop a deeper understanding of the material and cultivate a love for learning.

"Creating Opportunities for All Students to Contribute in the Classroom"

Ensuring that all students have the chance to contribute in the classroom is vital for fostering an inclusive and engaging learning environment. By implementing strategies that promote participation, educators can help every student feel valued and heard.

Use Diverse Teaching Methods

- **Varied Instructional Strategies**: Incorporate a **mix of lectures, discussions, hands-on activities, and multimedia presentations.** Different students respond better to different methods, so variety can cater to diverse learning styles.
- **Differentiated Instruction**: Tailor tasks and materials to meet the varied needs of students. Providing options allows students to engage with content in ways that resonate with them.

Establish Inclusive Norms

- **Set Ground Rules**: Create a classroom culture where respect and inclusion are prioritized. Establish norms that encourage students to listen actively and value each other's contributions.
- **Encourage Risk-Taking**: Make it clear that mistakes are part of the learning process. Encourage students to share their thoughts without fear of judgment.

Implement Structured Participation Techniques

- **Think-Pair-Share**: Give students time to think individually, discuss their ideas with a partner, and then share with the class. This structured approach allows all students to articulate their thoughts in a supportive environment.

- **Rotating Roles in Group Work**: In group settings, assign different roles to each student (e.g., facilitator, note-taker, and presenter). This ensures that everyone has a specific responsibility and a chance to contribute.

Incorporate Technology

- **Online Discussion Boards**: Use platforms like Google Classroom or Padlet to facilitate discussions outside of class. This allows students who may be hesitant to speak up in person to share their thoughts.
- **Interactive Polls and Surveys**: Tools like Mentimeter or Poll Everywhere can be used to gather input from all students quickly, making it easier for quieter students to participate.

Provide Choices and Autonomy

- **Choice in Topics**: Allow students to select topics for projects or presentations based on their interests. When students have a say in what they learn, they are more likely to engage.
- **Flexible Assignment Formats**: Give students options for how they demonstrate their understanding, such as **through written reports, videos, or artistic presentations.**

Encourage Peer Collaboration

- **Peer Teaching**: Organize opportunities for students to teach each other. This not only reinforces their own understanding but also values their input.
- **Group Discussions**: Foster small group discussions where every student is encouraged to share their ideas. This smaller setting can be less intimidating for some students.

Regularly Solicit Feedback

- **Feedback Forms**: Use anonymous feedback forms to gauge student comfort levels and preferences regarding participation. This helps identify barriers to involvement and provides insights for improvement.

- **Reflective Journals**: Encourage students to **keep journals where they reflect on their learning experiences and contributions.** This can help them articulate their thoughts and feel more connected to the material.

Utilize Non-Verbal Participation

- **Interactive Activities**: Incorporate activities that allow for non-verbal participation, such as using cards for responses or interactive games that don't rely solely on verbal communication.
- **Movement-Based Learning**: Use physical activities or gestures (e.g., thumbs up/down) to gauge understanding and keep students engaged without requiring verbal contributions.

Recognize and Celebrate Contributions

- **Highlight Efforts**: Acknowledge student contributions **publicly, whether through praise, sharing work, or celebrating successes.** Recognition fosters a sense of belonging and encourages future participation.
- **Create a Class Culture of Appreciation**: Encourage students to express appreciation for their peers' contributions. This can be done through "appreciation circles" or shout-outs during class.

Creating opportunities for all students to contribute in the classroom is essential for fostering an inclusive and dynamic learning environment. **By using diverse teaching methods, establishing inclusive norms, implementing structured participation techniques, incorporating technology, providing choices, encouraging peer collaboration, soliciting feedback, utilizing non-verbal participation, and recognizing contributions, educators can ensure that every student feels valued and engaged.** When students have the chance to share their voices, they are more likely to develop confidence, deepen their understanding, and foster a sense of community within the classroom.

"Strategies for Addressing Disengaged or Reluctant Learners"

Engaging disengaged or reluctant learners can be a challenge, but with targeted strategies, educators can foster interest and participation.

Build Strong Relationships

- **Personal Connections**: Take time to get to know your **students' interests, backgrounds, and challenges**. Building rapport can help students feel valued and understood.
- **One-on-One Conversations**: Engage **in informal discussions with reluctant learners to understand their perspectives and barriers to engagement**. Showing genuine interest can motivate them to participate.

Create a Positive Classroom Environment

- **Safe Space for Expression**: Foster an inclusive atmosphere **where students feel safe to express their thoughts without fear of judgment.** Encourage respect and open dialogue among peers.
- **Encourage a Growth Mindset**: Promote the **idea that effort and persistence lead to improvement. Celebrate small successes to help students recognize their progress.**

Make Learning Relevant

- **Connect to Interests**: Tailor lessons to relate to students' interests and real-life experiences. When students see the relevance of what they're learning, they are more likely to engage.
- **Incorporate Current Events**: Use **news stories or contemporary issues to spark discussions**. Relating content to the world outside the classroom can capture students' attention.

Incorporate Active Learning Techniques

- **Hands-On Activities**: Use interactive and experiential learning activities that allow students to engage physically and mentally. This could include experiments, projects, or role-playing.
- **Group Work**: Facilitate small group discussions or collaborative projects to encourage peer interaction. Students may feel more comfortable participating in a smaller setting.

Provide Choice and Autonomy

- **Choice in Assignments**: Allow students to choose topics or formats for their assignments. When they have a say in their learning, they are more likely to invest in it.
- **Flexible Learning Paths**: Offer different pathways for students to achieve learning goals, accommodating various interests and strengths.

Utilize Technology

- **Engaging Digital Tools**: Integrate educational apps, games, or online discussions that capture students' interest. Technology can make learning more interactive and appealing.
- **Flipped Classroom Models**: Provide instructional materials online for students to explore at their own pace, using class time for active discussions and hands-on activities.

Set Clear Goals and Expectations

- **Specific Learning Objectives**: Clearly outline the goals for each lesson, so students know what is expected. Breaking down tasks into manageable steps can reduce overwhelm.
- **Personalized Goals**: Help students set individualized goals based on their strengths and areas for improvement. Regularly revisit these goals to monitor progress.

Offer Support and Scaffolding

- **Additional Resources: Provide extra help or resources for students who may be struggling.** This could include tutoring, study groups, or access to online materials.
- **Scaffolded Instruction**: Break down **complex tasks into smaller, manageable components.** Gradually reduce support as students become more confident.

Incorporate Reflection

- **Reflective Journals**: Encourage students to keep journals where they can reflect on their learning experiences. This practice can help them articulate their thoughts and feelings about the material.
- **Feedback Sessions**: Regularly solicit feedback on what is working and what isn't. This helps student's feel heard and can provide valuable insights for improving engagement.

Celebrate Successes

- **Recognize Achievements**: Celebrate individual and group accomplishments, no matter how small. Acknowledgment fosters motivation and reinforces positive behaviors.
- **Peer Recognition**: Create opportunities for students to recognize each other's contributions. This can build a sense of community and encourage reluctant learners to participate.

Addressing disengaged or reluctant learners requires a multifaceted approach. **By building strong relationships, creating a positive classroom environment, making learning relevant, incorporating active learning techniques, providing choice, utilizing technology, setting clear goals, offering support, incorporating reflection, and celebrating successes, educators can effectively engage all stude**nts. With patience and persistence, teachers can help reluctant learners find their voice and develop a genuine interest in their education.

Chapter 9

Involving Students in Classroom Management

> ***"Teaching is a calling too. And I've always thought that teachers in their way are holy — angels leading their flocks out of the darkness."***
> *— Jeannette Walls, "Half Broke Horses"*

Involving students in classroom management fosters a sense of ownership, responsibility, and community within the classroom. When students participate in shaping the rules and procedures that govern their learning environment, they are more likely to engage actively and positively.

Co-creating Classroom Rules

- **Collaborative Rule-Making**: At the beginning of the school year or term, **engage students in a discussion to develop classroom rules together**. This process encourages buy-in and helps students feel that their voices matter.
- **Focus on Values**: Ask students to identify the values they believe are important for a positive classroom environment. Use these values as a foundation for the rules.

Establishing Procedures Together

- **Input on Routines**: Involve students in creating procedures for daily routines, such as how to transition between activities or how to submit assignments. When students help design these processes, they are more likely to follow them.
- **Role Assignments**: Allow students to take on specific roles related to classroom management, such as line leaders or materials managers. This gives them a sense of responsibility and ownership.

Encouraging Student Voice

- **Feedback Mechanisms**: Create opportunities for students to provide feedback on classroom management practices. This can be done through surveys, suggestion boxes, or open discussions.
- **Student-Led Discussions**: Facilitate regular discussions where students can voice their concerns, share ideas, and propose changes to classroom management strategies.

Setting Goals Together

- **Classroom Goals**: Collaboratively **set goals for the class, such as academic achievements or behavior expectations**. Involving students in goal-setting helps them take ownership of their learning environment.
- **Reflection on Progress**: Regularly review and reflect on progress toward these goals. This encourages accountability and allows students to see the impact of their contributions.

Peer Mediation and Conflict Resolution

- **Student Mediators**: Train students to act as **peer mediators to help resolve conflicts among classmates.** This not only empowers students but also fosters a sense of community and cooperation.
- **Conflict Resolution Workshops**: Involve **students in workshops that teach conflict resolution strategies**. This equips them with the skills to manage disagreements constructively.

Incorporating Student Interests

- **Interest-Based Activities**: Allow students to suggest activities or topics related to the curriculum. When learning is connected to their interests, students are more likely to be engaged and participate actively.
- **Thematic Units**: Involve students in selecting **themes for project-based learning or unit studies, giving them a voice in their educational experiences.**

Creating a Class Charter

- **Classroom Constitution**: Develop a class charter that **outlines the rights and responsibilities of students.** Involving them in this process fosters a sense of belonging and shared responsibility.
- **Commitment to the Charter**: Have **students sign the charter as a commitment to upholding the agreed-upon values and rules.** This reinforces accountability.

Recognizing Contributions

- **Celebrating Achievements: Acknowledge and celebrate instances where students demonstrate responsibility and positive behavior. Recognizing their contributions reinforces their role in classroom management.**
- **Peer Recognition**: Create a system where **students can recognize and appreciate each other's efforts in maintaining a positive classroom environment.**

Involving students in classroom management is crucial for creating an inclusive and effective learning environment. **By co-creating rules and procedures, encouraging student voice, setting goals together, training peer mediators, incorporating student interests, developing a class charter, and recognizing contributions, educators can foster a sense of ownership and responsibility among students.** When students feel that they have a stake in their classroom community, they are more likely to engage, cooperate, and contribute positively to the learning experience.

"Empowering Students in the Classroom"

Empowering students is essential for fostering independence, confidence, and a sense of ownership over their learning. When students feel empowered, they are more likely **to engage actively, take initiative, and develop critical thinking skills.**

Encourage Student Voice

- **Feedback Opportunities**: Create regular channels for students to express their thoughts and opinions about the learning environment, activities, and teaching methods. This could include surveys, suggestion boxes, or class discussions.
- **Student-Led Conferences**: Allow students to take the **lead in parent-teacher conferences, presenting their work and reflecting on their progress**. This practice enhances their sense of agency and accountability.

Promote Autonomy

- **Choice in Learning**: Provide **options in assignments, projects, and topics of study**. Allowing students to choose how they demonstrate their understanding fosters a sense of control over their education.
- **Self-Paced Learning**: **Implement self-paced activities or learning paths where students can progress according to their individual needs and interests.** This encourages ownership of their learning journey.

Set High Expectations

- **Challenge Students**: Set ambitious yet **achievable goals for students.** Encouraging them to reach for high standards helps build resilience and a growth mindset.
- **Celebrate Efforts and Progress**: Recognize and celebrate not just the outcomes but also the effort and progress students make toward their goals. This reinforces their belief in their capabilities.

Teach Goal-Setting Skills

- **Personalized Goals**: Help students set specific, measurable, achievable, relevant, and time-bound **(SMART) goals.** This teaches them how to plan and strive for their objectives.
- **Regular Reflection**: Incorporate reflection sessions where students assess their progress toward their goals. This practice promotes self-awareness and accountability.

Foster Critical Thinking

- **Open-Ended Questions**: Encourage students to engage with complex, open-ended questions that require deeper thinking and exploration. This cultivates their analytical skills and confidence in expressing their thoughts.
- **Problem-Based Learning**: Present real-world problems for students to solve collaboratively. This approach encourages innovation and empowers them to take ownership of their learning.

Encourage Collaboration

- **Peer Learning**: Facilitate opportunities for students to work together, share ideas, and learn from one another. Collaborative projects build a sense of community and enhance communication skills.
- **Student-Led Groups**: Allow students to form their own study groups or clubs based on their interests. This encourages initiative and leadership skills.

Integrate Technology

- **Digital Tools for Collaboration**: Use platforms like Google Classroom, Padlet, or collaborative apps to enhance group work and communication. Technology can facilitate student-driven projects and discussions.

- **Online Portfolios**: Encourage students to create digital portfolios showcasing their work and progress. This not only highlights their achievements but also allows them to take ownership of their learning journey.

Provide Constructive Feedback

- **Timely and Specific Feedback**: Offer constructive feedback that focuses on strengths and areas for improvement. Encourage students to use feedback as a tool for growth rather than criticism.
- **Peer Feedback**: Implement peer review sessions where students give and receive feedback on each other's work. This fosters a collaborative learning environment and enhances critical thinking.

Encourage Initiative and Responsibility

- **Classroom Jobs**: Assign responsibilities within the classroom, such as managing materials or leading discussions. These roles empower students and promote accountability.
- **Project Ownership**: Allow students to take the lead on projects, including planning, executing, and presenting their work. This fosters a sense of ownership and pride in their achievements.

Empowering students in the classroom is crucial for fostering engagement, independence, and a lifelong love for learning. **By encouraging student voice, promoting autonomy, setting high expectations, teaching goal-setting skills, fostering critical thinking, encouraging collaboration, integrating technology, providing constructive feedback, and encouraging initiative, educators can create an environment where students feel valued and capable.** When students are empowered, they become active participants in their education, ready to tackle challenges and pursue their interests with confidence.

"Techniques for Giving Students a Voice in the Classroom"

Empowering students to express their thoughts, opinions, and ideas is essential for fostering an inclusive and dynamic learning environment.

Create a Safe and Inclusive Environment

- **Establish Trust**: Build relationships with students so they feel comfortable sharing their thoughts. Encourage respect and active listening among peers.
- **Celebrate Diversity**: Acknowledge and honor diverse perspectives and backgrounds. Promote an atmosphere where all voices are valued.

Implement Structured Discussions

- **Socratic Seminars**: Use open-ended questions to facilitate student-led discussions. Encourage students to engage with each other's ideas and build on them, fostering deeper dialogue.
- **Think-Pair-Share**: Allow students to think individually about a question, discuss it with a partner, and then share their thoughts with the larger group. This structure encourages participation from all students.

Utilize Technology for Engagement

- **Digital Platforms**: Use tools like Google Classroom or Padlet for online discussions. This can be especially helpful for students who may be hesitant to speak up in person.
- **Interactive Polls and Surveys**: Utilize apps like Mentimeter or Poll Everywhere to gather student opinions and feedback in real-time, ensuring everyone has a chance to contribute.

Encourage Student-Led Activities

- **Student-Led Conferences**: Allow students to take the lead during parent-teacher conferences, presenting their work and reflecting on their progress.
- **Peer Teaching**: Create opportunities for students to teach their peers on topics they are passionate about. This fosters confidence and encourages them to share their knowledge.

Facilitate Reflection

- **Reflective Journals**: Encourage students to maintain journals where they can articulate their thoughts, feelings, and reflections on their learning experiences.
- **Feedback Sessions**: Regularly hold sessions where students can provide feedback on classroom activities and discuss what works for them and what doesn't.

Incorporate Student Interests

- **Interest Surveys**: Conduct surveys at the beginning of the year to learn about students' interests and passions. Use this information to inform lesson planning and activities.
- **Choice in Projects**: Provide options for projects or topics, allowing students to explore areas they find compelling. This increases engagement and investment in their learning.

Create a Class Constitution

- **Collaborative Rule-Making**: Involve students in developing a classroom charter that outlines their rights and responsibilities. This gives them ownership over the classroom culture.
- **Regular Revisions**: Encourage students to revisit and revise the charter as needed, fostering a sense of agency and adaptability.

Promote Collaborative Learning

- **Group Work**: Facilitate small group discussions or projects that encourage students to share their ideas and collaborate. This setting can be less intimidating for some students.
- **Peer Feedback**: Implement peer review processes where students give and receive feedback on each other's work, promoting collaboration and constructive criticism.

Encourage Questions

- **Question-Driven Learning**: Foster a culture where questions are welcomed and valued. Encourage students to ask questions about the material and each other's ideas.
- **Question Stems**: Provide sentence starters to help students formulate their inquiries. This can assist those who may struggle to articulate their thoughts.

Recognize Contributions

- **Celebrate Participation**: Acknowledge student contributions publicly, whether through praise, sharing work, or celebrating successes. Recognition reinforces the importance of their voice.
- **Peer Recognition Programs**: Create opportunities for students to recognize and appreciate each other's efforts, further promoting a supportive classroom environment.

Giving students a voice in the classroom is crucial for fostering engagement, confidence, and a sense of belonging. **By creating a safe environment, implementing structured discussions, utilizing technology, encouraging student-led activities, facilitating reflection, incorporating student interests, creating a class constitution, promoting collaborative learning, encouraging questions, and recognizing contributions, educators can empower students to express themselves and take an active role in their education.** When students feel heard and valued, they are more likely to engage deeply in the learning process and develop a love for learning that extends beyond the classroom.

"Encouraging Self-Regulation and Responsibility in Students"

Fostering self-regulation and responsibility in students is crucial for their academic success and personal growth. **When students learn to manage their emotions, behaviors, and academic tasks, they become more independent and engaged learners.**

Set Clear Expectations

- **Define Goals Together**: Collaborate with **students to establish clear, achievable goals for behavior and academic performance**. This gives them **ownership** of their learning journey.
- **Communicate Standards**: Clearly **outline classroom rules and procedures**. Make sure students understand the importance of these expectations for maintaining a positive learning environment.

Teach Self-Monitoring Skills

- **Reflection Journals**: Encourage students to keep journals where they can reflect on their behavior, progress, and challenges. This practice promotes self-awareness and critical thinking.
- **Checklists and Rubrics**: Provide checklists or rubrics for assignments, allowing students to assess their own work before submission. This encourages them to take responsibility for their learning.

Incorporate Goal-Setting Activities

- **SMART Goals**: Teach students to set SMART (**Specific, Measurable, Achievable, Relevant, Time-bound**) goals for their academic and personal growth. Regularly revisit these goals to track progress.
- **Visual Goal Trackers**: Use visual **aids like charts or graphs** to help students monitor their progress. This can make goal achievement more tangible and motivating.

Encourage Time Management

- **Planning Tools**: Provide tools such as **planners or digital calendars** to help students organize their assignments and manage their time effectively.
- **Chunking Tasks**: Teach students **to break larger projects into smaller**, manageable tasks. This makes daunting assignments more approachable and fosters a sense of accomplishment.

Promote a Growth Mindset

- **Teach Resilience**: Encourage students to **view challenges as opportunities for growth rather than obstacles.** Share stories of perseverance to inspire them.
- **Focus on Effort**: Emphasize **the importance of effort and improvement over perfection.** Recognizing progress can help students develop resilience and motivation.

Provide Opportunities for Choice

- **Choice in Assignments**: Allow students to choose how they complete assignments or projects. This autonomy encourages them to take responsibility for their learning.
- **Flexible Learning Paths**: Offer different pathways for achieving learning objectives. Students can explore topics that interest them, enhancing their engagement and responsibility.

Foster a Supportive Classroom Environment

- **Encourage Peer Support**: Create a culture of collaboration where students can help each other. Peer encouragement fosters responsibility and builds a sense of community.
- **Model Self-Regulation**: Demonstrate self-regulation and responsibility in your own behavior. Share strategies you use to manage your tasks and emotions.

Incorporate Problem-Solving Activities

- **Real-World Scenarios**: Present students with real-life problems to solve collaboratively. This encourages critical thinking and allows them to practice responsibility in decision-making.
- **Role-Playing**: Use role-playing exercises to help students navigate situations that require self-regulation and responsibility. This can enhance their social-emotional skills.

Encourage Reflection and Feedback

- **Regular Check-Ins**: Hold regular one-on-one or small group check-ins to discuss progress and areas for improvement. This promotes accountability and provides an opportunity for feedback.
- **Peer Feedback**: Implement peer review processes where students can offer constructive feedback on each other's work. This fosters responsibility for both their own and others' learning.

Recognize and Celebrate Responsibility

- **Acknowledge Efforts**: Recognize students who demonstrate self-regulation and responsibility, whether through verbal praise or rewards. Celebrating these behaviors reinforces their importance.
- **Classroom Responsibilities**: Assign classroom jobs or responsibilities to students. Giving them specific roles fosters a sense of ownership and accountability.

Encouraging self-regulation and responsibility in students is vital for their personal and academic development. **By setting clear expectations, teaching self-monitoring skills, incorporating goal-setting activities, promoting time management, fostering a growth mindset, providing opportunities for choice, creating a supportive environment, incorporating problem-solving activities, encouraging reflection, and recognizing responsible behaviors, educators can help students develop these essential skills**. When students learn to manage their emotions and behaviors and take responsibility for their learning, they become more empowered and engaged individuals, ready to tackle challenges both inside and outside the classroom.

"Peer Mediation and Conflict Resolution in the Classroom"

Peer mediation and conflict resolution are vital components of a positive classroom environment. **These approaches empower students to handle disagreements constructively, develop critical social-emotional skills, and foster a sense of community.**

Understanding Peer Mediation

- **Definition**: Peer mediation involves students helping their peers resolve conflicts through structured dialogue, guided by trained mediators. This process encourages collaboration and understanding.
- **Benefits**: It promotes problem-solving skills, empathy, and accountability while reducing bullying and disruptive behavior.

Training Peer Mediators

- **Selection Process**: Identify and select students who demonstrate strong communication skills, empathy, and a willingness to help others. Consider diversity in age, background, and social dynamics.
- **Training Workshops**: Provide training sessions on conflict resolution techniques, active listening, and mediation strategies. Role-playing scenarios can help students practice their skills.
- **Ongoing Support**: Offer continuous support and feedback for peer mediators, allowing them to refine their skills and stay motivated.

Creating a Mediation Program

- **Establish Clear Procedures**: Develop a structured mediation process that outlines the steps students should follow when they wish to seek mediation. This can include how to request a mediator and what to expect during the process.

- **Confidentiality and Safety**: Ensure that students feel safe and that their discussions will remain confidential. This encourages open communication during mediation sessions.

Implementing Conflict Resolution Strategies

- **Teaching Conflict Resolution Skills**: Integrate lessons on conflict resolution into the curriculum, focusing on techniques like active listening, assertive communication, and empathy.

- **Role-Playing Scenarios**: Use role-playing exercises to help students practice handling conflicts in a safe and controlled environment. This allows them to experiment with different strategies.

Encouraging Open Communication

- **Facilitate Open Discussions**: Create an environment where students feel comfortable discussing their feelings and concerns. Regularly check in with students about their experiences and feelings.

- **Classroom Meetings**: Hold regular classroom meetings where students can voice concerns and discuss issues collectively. This promotes transparency and community building.

Promoting Empathy and Understanding

- **Empathy Exercises**: Incorporate activities that encourage students to see situations from others' perspectives. This can deepen their understanding of conflicts and enhance their mediation skills.

- **Storytelling**: Use stories or scenarios to illustrate conflict resolution concepts. Discuss how characters might handle conflicts and the potential outcomes of their choices.

Encouraging Self-Reflection

- **Reflection Journals**: Encourage students to maintain journals where they can reflect on their conflicts, emotions, and the resolution process. This practice promotes self-awareness and personal growth.
- **Feedback Sessions**: After mediation sessions, provide opportunities for peer mediators and participants to reflect on what worked, what didn't, and how they can improve in the future.

Recognizing and Celebrating Successes

- **Acknowledge Positive Outcomes**: Recognize and celebrate successful resolutions to conflicts, whether through verbal praise, certificates, or classroom displays. This reinforces the value of mediation and conflict resolution.
- **Peer Recognition Programs**: Create opportunities for students to acknowledge each other's efforts in resolving conflicts and supporting one another.

Implementing peer mediation and conflict resolution strategies in the classroom is essential for fostering a positive and collaborative learning environment. **By training peer mediators, establishing clear procedures, teaching conflict resolution skills, encouraging open communication, promoting empathy, and recognizing successes, educators can empower students to take charge of their social interactions. These skills not only help students navigate conflicts effectively but also prepare them for successful relationships and teamwork in the future**. Ultimately, a strong emphasis on peer mediation contributes to a more harmonious and productive classroom community.

"Teaching Conflict Resolution Skills to Students"

Teaching conflict resolution skills is essential for helping students navigate disagreements effectively and build positive relationships. These skills not only enhance social-emotional development but also foster a collaborative learning environment.

Introduce the Concept of Conflict

- **Define Conflict**: Begin by discussing what conflict is and why it occurs. Use relatable examples to illustrate common sources of conflict among students, such as misunderstandings or differing opinions.
- **Normalize Conflict**: Emphasize that conflict is a natural part of relationships and can be resolved constructively. Encourage students to view conflict as an opportunity for growth and learning.

Teach Active Listening

- **Importance of Listening**: Explain that effective conflict resolution starts with listening. Teach students **the value of hearing others' perspectives before responding.**
- **Active Listening Exercises**: Use activities that promote active listening, such as:
    - **Paraphrasing**: Have students practice summarizing what a partner has said to ensure understanding.
    - **Listening Pairs**: In pairs, one student shares their thoughts while the other listens without interrupting and then switches roles.

Model Effective Communication

- **Use "I" Statements**: Teach students to express their feelings and needs using "I" statements (e.g., "I feel upset when..."). This approach helps prevent blame and defensiveness.

- **Role-Playing Scenarios**: Create role-playing exercises where students practice using "I" statements to address conflicts. This helps them learn to communicate feelings assertively yet respectfully.

Teach Problem-Solving Techniques

- **Identify the Problem**: Guide students in identifying the root cause of a conflict. Encourage them to articulate the issue clearly.
- **Brainstorm Solutions**: Involve students in brainstorming potential solutions to the conflict. Emphasize the importance of considering various perspectives and outcomes.
- **Evaluate Options**: Teach students to evaluate the pros and cons of each solution and choose the most effective one collaboratively.

Encourage Empathy

- **Perspective-Taking Activities**: Use activities that promote empathy, such as role-reversal exercises where students act out each other's viewpoints during a conflict.
- **Empathy Discussions**: Discuss scenarios and ask students how each person might be feeling. Encourage them to consider the emotions and motivations of others involved.

Teach Negotiation Skills

- **Negotiation Role-Playing**: Set up role-playing scenarios where students practice negotiating resolutions to conflicts. This helps them develop the skills to find common ground.
- **Compromise Techniques**: Teach students the importance of compromise and flexibility. Encourage them to look for solutions that satisfy everyone involved.

Implement Conflict Resolution Frameworks

Step-by-Step Framework: Introduce a simple conflict resolution framework, such as:

1. **Identify the Conflict**: What is the issue?
2. **Understand All Perspectives**: Listen to everyone involved.
3. **Brainstorm Solutions**: What can be done?
4. **Agree on a Solution**: Decide on a way forward.
5. **Follow Up**: Check in to ensure the solution is working.

Visual Aids: Use posters or charts to display this framework, making it easy for students to reference when conflicts arise.

Create Opportunities for Practice

- **Conflict Scenarios**: Present students with hypothetical conflict scenarios and have them work in groups to resolve them using the skills learned.

- **Peer Mediation Programs**: Encourage students to participate in peer mediation, allowing them to practice their conflict resolution skills in real situations.

Reflect on Experiences

- **Debriefing Sessions**: After resolving a conflict or participating in mediation, hold debriefing sessions where students reflect on what worked well and what could be improved.

- **Self-Assessment**: Encourage students to assess their conflict resolution skills and set personal goals for improvement.

Reinforce Positive Behavior

- **Recognition and Rewards**: Acknowledge students who effectively use conflict resolution skills. This can motivate others to develop similar behaviors.

- **Create a Supportive Environment**: Foster a classroom culture that values collaboration, respect, and open communication, reinforcing the importance of conflict resolution skills.

Teaching conflict resolution skills is a vital part of students' social-emotional development. **By introducing the concept of conflict, teaching active listening, effective communication, problem-solving, empathy, negotiation, and implementing frameworks, educators** can equip students with the tools they need to navigate disagreements constructively. Creating opportunities for practice and reflection reinforces these skills, fostering a harmonious and collaborative classroom environment where students feel empowered to resolve conflicts positively.

Chapter 10

Collaboration with Families in Education

> ***"A teacher takes a hand, opens a mind, and touches a heart." "Educators are the architects of the future." "Teachers change the world one student at a time." "The influence of a good teacher can never be erased."***
>
> *— Anonymous*

Collaboration with families is a crucial aspect of creating a supportive and effective educational environment. **Engaging families in the educational process fosters stronger connections between home and school, enhances student learning, and promotes a sense of community**.

Establish Open Communication

- **Regular Updates**: Use newsletters, emails, or school apps to keep families informed about classroom activities, upcoming events, and important announcements.
- **Two-Way Communication**: Encourage families to share their thoughts and concerns. Provide opportunities for feedback through surveys, suggestion boxes, or regular check-ins.

Create Welcoming Environments

- **Inclusive School Culture**: Make families feel welcome by creating an inclusive atmosphere that respects diverse backgrounds and perspectives. This can be reflected in school events, materials, and communication styles.
- **Family Events**: Host events such as open houses, family nights, or workshops that invite families to participate in the school community and engage with educators.

Encourage Parental Involvement

- **Volunteer Opportunities**: Offer various ways for families to get involved, whether through classroom assistance, organizing events, or participating in school committees.
- **Family Learning Workshops**: Provide workshops on topics such as academic support, social-emotional learning, or literacy strategies, equipping families with tools to help their children at home.

Build Trusting Relationships

- **Personal Connections**: Take the time to build relationships with families. Make an effort to learn about their interests, concerns, and backgrounds to foster a sense of trust.
- **Positive Communication**: Share positive news about students' progress and achievements regularly. This helps families feel valued and more connected to the school.

Involve Families in Decision-Making

- **Parent Advisory Committees**: Create committees that involve parents in school decision-making processes, ensuring their voices are heard in matters affecting their children's education.
- **Collaborative Goal-Setting**: Work with families to set academic and behavioral goals for their children. This collaborative approach empowers families and aligns home and school expectations.

Utilize Technology

- **Communication Platforms**: Use digital platforms such as school websites, social media, or apps to share information and updates. This can make communication more accessible and efficient.
- **Online Resources**: Provide families with access to online resources and tools that support learning at home, such as educational websites or homework help.

Support Diverse Families

- **Cultural Competence**: Acknowledge and respect the diverse cultural backgrounds of families. Tailor communication and involvement strategies to meet their unique needs.
- **Language Accessibility**: Provide translation services or materials in multiple languages to ensure that all families can engage effectively with the school.

Address Concerns and Challenges

- **Open-Door Policy**: Encourage families to reach out with concerns. Be responsive and willing to work collaboratively to address issues that may arise.
- **Conflict Resolution**: Establish clear processes for resolving conflicts or misunderstandings. This helps maintain positive relationships and a supportive environment.

Celebrate Successes Together

- **Acknowledge Achievements**: Celebrate student successes in collaboration with families. This can include award ceremonies, recognition events, or showcasing student work.
- **Community Recognition**: Highlight family contributions to the school community in newsletters or at events, reinforcing the importance of their involvement.

Evaluate and Reflect

- **Feedback on Collaboration**: Regularly seek feedback from families about their experiences and perceptions of collaboration. Use this information to improve practices.
- **Reflect on Practices**: Educators should reflect on their collaboration efforts, considering what works well and where improvements can be made to strengthen family partnerships.

Collaboration with families is essential for fostering a supportive and enriching educational environment. **By establishing open communication, creating welcoming spaces, encouraging parental involvement, building trusting relationships, involving families in decision-making, utilizing technology, supporting diverse families, addressing concerns, celebrating successes, and continuously evaluating practices, educators can strengthen partnerships with families.** These efforts enhance student learning and create a cohesive community where families and schools work together to support students' growth and success.

"Engaging Parents in Classroom Management"

Engaging parents in classroom management is vital for creating a supportive and cohesive educational environment. When parents and teachers collaborate, it enhances student behavior, promotes consistency, and fosters a sense of community. Here are effective strategies for involving parents in classroom management:

Establish Open Lines of Communication

- **Regular Updates**: Provide parents with consistent updates about classroom rules, expectations, and ongoing behavior management strategies through newsletters, emails, or parent portals.
- **Two-Way Communication**: Encourage parents to share their insights, concerns, and observations about their child's behavior at home. Use surveys or informal check-ins to gather feedback.

Involve Parents in Setting Expectations

- **Collaborative Rule-Making**: Invite parents to participate in developing classroom rules and expectations. This can be done through surveys or discussions at parent meetings, ensuring that family values align with classroom guidelines.
- **Parent Workshops**: Host workshops where parents can learn about classroom management strategies and the importance of consistency between home and school.

Share Behavior Expectations and Strategies

- **Clear Guidelines**: Clearly communicate the classroom behavior expectations to parents, ensuring they understand how they can reinforce these expectations at home.
- **Behavior Contracts**: Consider implementing behavior contracts that involve both students and parents. This formalizes expectations and encourages accountability.

Encourage Parental Involvement in Reinforcement

- **Home Reinforcement Strategies**: Share effective strategies that parents can use at home to reinforce positive behavior. This can include specific praise, rewards, or routines that mirror classroom expectations.

- **Behavior Tracking**: Provide tools, such as charts or journals, for parents to track their child's behavior at home, fostering a sense of partnership and accountability.

Create Opportunities for Parent Participation

- **Classroom Volunteer Opportunities**: Encourage parents to volunteer in the classroom. Their presence can positively influence student behavior and reinforce classroom expectations.

- **Involvement in Events**: Invite parents to participate in classroom events, such as behavior recognition ceremonies or theme days, fostering a sense of community and shared responsibility.

Foster a Supportive Environment

- **Recognize Contributions**: Acknowledge and celebrate the involvement of parents in supporting classroom management. This can include recognizing their efforts in newsletters or during school events.

- **Build Trusting Relationships**: Take the time to build positive relationships with parents. Understanding their perspectives can enhance cooperation and support for classroom management efforts.

Provide Resources and Training

- **Parent Education Programs**: Offer workshops or informational sessions focused on behavior management techniques that parents can apply at home, such as effective discipline strategies or communication skills.

- **Resource Materials**: Distribute materials that provide tips for managing behavior, conflict resolution, and fostering positive interactions at home.

Solicit Feedback and Input

- **Parent Surveys**: Regularly conduct surveys to gather parents' input on classroom management practices and their effectiveness. Use this feedback to make necessary adjustments.
- **Suggestion Box**: Implement a suggestion box for parents to anonymously share their thoughts or concerns about classroom management strategies.

Communicate About Behavioral Issues

- **Timely Communication**: Notify parents promptly about any behavioral issues their child may be facing. Be clear and constructive, focusing on solutions rather than just the problems.
- **Collaborative Problem-Solving**: Involve parents in discussions about behavioral challenges and collaboratively develop strategies to address them. This approach reinforces the idea that home and school are working together for the child's benefit.

Celebrate Successes Together

- **Recognize Achievements**: Share and celebrate student successes in managing behavior, both at school and at home. This can include highlighting positive behaviors during meetings or through newsletters.
- **Family Involvement in Celebrations**: Invite parents to participate in celebrations for positive behavior, such as reward days or recognition ceremonies, reinforcing the importance of their involvement.

Engaging parents in classroom management is crucial for creating a unified approach to behavior expectations and student success. **By establishing open communication, involving parents in setting expectations, sharing strategies, encouraging participation, and providing resources, educators can foster a strong partnership with families**. This collaboration enhances the overall learning environment, supports student behavior, and builds a community where everyone shares responsibility for student development.

"Strategies for Communicating with Families about Classroom Expectations"

Effective communication with families about classroom expectations is essential for fostering a supportive learning environment. Clear communication helps ensure that parents understand the rules, procedures, and values being taught in the classroom.

Create a Welcome Packet

- **Comprehensive Overview**: At the beginning of the school year, provide a welcome packet that includes a letter introducing yourself, a summary of classroom expectations, and an outline of important policies and procedures.
- **Accessible Language**: Use clear and straightforward language, avoiding educational jargon to ensure all parents can easily understand the information.

Utilize Multiple Communication Channels

- **Diverse Formats**: Use a combination of newsletters, emails, text messages, and school apps to reach families. Different families may prefer different communication methods.
- **Visual Aids**: Incorporate visuals like infographics or charts to illustrate expectations. This can make information more engaging and easier to digest.

Host Parent Orientation Meetings

- **Interactive Sessions**: Organize orientation meetings at the start of the year to discuss classroom expectations in detail. Use this time to engage parents through Q&A sessions.
- **Workshops**: Offer workshops that explain how classroom expectations align with school values and academic goals, allowing for deeper understanding and discussion.

Establish Regular Updates

- **Consistent Communication**: Send regular updates (weekly or bi-weekly) that highlight key classroom activities reinforce expectations, and celebrate student successes.
- **Behavior Reports**: Include information about individual student progress regarding behavior and adherence to classroom rules, reinforcing accountability.

Create a Classroom Website or Blog

- **Online Resource**: Develop a classroom website or blog where families can easily access information about expectations, assignments, and important dates.
- **Interactive Features**: Allow parents to leave comments or ask questions online, fostering an ongoing dialogue about classroom matters.

Use Family Conferences

- **Personalized Meetings**: Schedule one-on-one conferences with families to discuss individual student behavior and expectations. This personalized approach can address specific concerns and build trust.
- **Goal Setting**: Collaborate with families to set behavior goals for their children, ensuring that everyone is on the same page regarding expectations.

Incorporate Feedback Mechanisms

- **Surveys and Questionnaires**: Distribute surveys to gather parent feedback on their understanding of classroom expectations and any areas where they need clarification.
- **Suggestion Boxes**: Create anonymous suggestion boxes for parents to share their thoughts or questions about classroom rules and procedures.

Use Visual Reminders in the Classroom

- **Post Expectations**: Display classroom rules and expectations prominently in the classroom. Consider providing families with a copy to reinforce what is being taught at home.
- **Visual Cues**: Use visual reminders, such as charts or posters, to illustrate expected behaviors, making them easier for students and families to remember.

Engage Students as Communicators

- **Student-Led Conferences**: Involve students in communicating classroom expectations by having them lead discussions during conferences, presenting what they have learned about behavior and rules.
- **Home Assignments**: Encourage students to share classroom expectations with their families as part of a homework assignment, facilitating discussion at home.

Celebrate Compliance and Successes

- **Highlight Positive Behavior**: Regularly communicate and celebrate instances of students adhering to classroom expectations, both to students and their families.
- **Recognition Programs**: Share success stories in newsletters or during meetings, reinforcing the importance of expectations and family involvement.

Communicating effectively with families about classroom expectations is key to building a strong partnership that supports student success. By using a variety of communication channels, hosting interactive meetings, providing regular updates, and incorporating feedback mechanisms, educators can ensure that parents are well-informed and engaged. This collaborative approach fosters a unified environment where expectations are understood and reinforced both at home and in the classroom.

"Importance of Family Support in Reinforcing Positive Behavior"

Family support plays a crucial role in reinforcing positive behavior in children and adolescents. When families actively engage in their children's educational journey and behavioral development, it creates a consistent environment that promotes learning and personal growth.

Consistency in Expectations

- **Unified Approach**: When families and schools work together to establish consistent expectations for behavior, children are more likely to understand and adhere to these guidelines. Consistency across environments reduces confusion and reinforces positive behaviors.
- **Reinforcement of Values**: Family support helps to reinforce the values and expectations set in the classroom, creating a coherent framework for children to follow.

Enhanced Motivation

- **Emotional Support**: Family encouragement boosts children's self-esteem and motivation. When families celebrate achievements and provide positive feedback, children are more inclined to engage in positive behaviors.
- **Increased Accountability**: Knowing that their families are involved and invested in their behavior encourages children to take responsibility for their actions.

Modeling Positive Behavior

- **Role Models**: Families serve as primary role models for children. When parents and guardians demonstrate positive behavior, such as effective communication and problem-solving, children are more likely to emulate these behaviors.

- **Behavioral Norms**: Consistent modeling of positive behavior at home helps establish behavioral norms that children carry into school and other social settings.

Strengthened Relationships

- **Building Trust**: Strong family support fosters trusting relationships between parents and children, which is essential for open communication about behavior and expectations.
- **Increased Engagement**: Engaged families are more likely to create a nurturing environment that encourages children to discuss their experiences and challenges, further supporting positive behavior.

Coping Strategies and Conflict Resolution

- **Emotional Guidance**: Families provide emotional support that helps children navigate conflicts and challenges. Teaching effective coping strategies at home equips children with the tools to handle difficulties positively.
- **Conflict Resolution Skills**: When families emphasize the importance of resolving conflicts constructively, children learn to apply these skills in school and social interactions.

Encouragement of Positive Activities

- **Participation in Activities**: Family involvement in extracurricular activities and community events encourages children to engage in positive social interactions and develop new skills.
- **Structured Environment**: Families that create structured environments for homework, chores, and leisure activities promote responsibility and positive behavior.

Effective Communication Channels

- **Open Dialogue**: Supportive families foster open lines of communication where children feel safe expressing their feelings and concerns. This communication is vital for addressing behavioral issues as they arise.
- **Feedback Loop**: Regular discussions between families and educators create a feedback loop that allows for collaborative problem-solving regarding behavioral challenges.

Celebrating Successes Together

- **Recognition of Achievements**: Families play a key role in recognizing and celebrating their children's accomplishments, no matter how small. This recognition reinforces the behaviors that led to success.
- **Positive Reinforcement**: Celebrating successes encourages children to continue engaging in positive behaviors, knowing their efforts are appreciated.

Community Building

- **Strengthening the Community**: When families support positive behavior collectively, it builds a sense of community and belonging, both at home and in school.
- **Shared Responsibility**: Involving families in reinforcing positive behavior creates a shared responsibility for children's development, enhancing cooperation between home and school.

Family support is essential in reinforcing positive behavior in children. **By fostering consistency, enhancing motivation, modeling positive behavior, and encouraging open communication, families create a nurturing environment that significantly impacts children's development.** When families and schools work collaboratively, they lay the foundation for children to thrive, ensuring that positive behaviors are recognized, reinforced, and celebrated both at home and in educational settings.

"Addressing Concerns Together: The Role of Family and Educator Collaboration"

Effective collaboration between families and educators is crucial for addressing concerns related to a child's behavior, academic performance, or social-emotional development. When families and schools work together, they can create a unified support system that fosters student success.

Open Lines of Communication

- **Regular Updates**: Establish consistent communication channels to keep families informed about their child's progress and any emerging concerns. This can include newsletters, emails, or phone calls.
- **Two-Way Communication**: Encourage families to share their observations and concerns about their child's behavior or academic performance. Create a safe space for open dialogue.

Schedule Regular Meetings

- **Parent-Teacher Conferences**: Organize regular conferences to discuss students' progress and address any concerns. Make these meetings a priority to foster strong relationships.
- **Check-Ins**: Offer informal check-ins throughout the year to discuss any immediate concerns and collaboratively develop strategies to support the child.

Collaborative Problem-Solving

- **Identify Concerns Together**: Work with families to clearly identify specific concerns regarding behavior or academics. Use data and examples to facilitate understanding.
- **Brainstorm Solutions**: Involve families in generating potential solutions. Collaborative brainstorming can lead to innovative strategies that consider both home and school contexts.

Establish Goals and Action Plans

- **Shared Goals**: Set mutual goals that reflect the concerns discussed. Ensure that these goals are specific, measurable, achievable, relevant, and time-bound (SMART).
- **Action Plans**: Develop a clear action plan that outlines the steps both educators and families will take to address the concerns. Assign responsibilities and establish timelines.

Monitor Progress Together

- **Regular Updates**: Keep families informed about their child's progress in relation to the agreed-upon goals. Provide regular updates and celebrate small successes along the way.
- **Adjust Strategies**: Be flexible and willing to adjust strategies as needed based on feedback from families and ongoing observations in the classroom.

Provide Resources and Support

- **Educational Resources**: Share resources, such as articles, workshops, or online tools, that can help families support their child's learning and behavior at home.
- **Referrals**: If needed, refer families to additional support services, such as counseling or tutoring, to address specific concerns more effectively.

Build Trust and Rapport

- **Positive Communication**: Foster a positive relationship by celebrating successes and maintaining a strengths-based approach when discussing concerns. This helps build trust and rapport.
- **Empathy and Understanding**: Approach concerns with empathy. Acknowledge the challenges families face and show that you value their input and perspective.

Engage the Child in the Process

- **Student Involvement**: Encourage students to take part in discussions about their behavior and academic goals. This empowers them and helps them understand the importance of collaboration.
- **Self-Advocacy Skills**: Teach students self-advocacy skills so they can express their feelings and concerns effectively, further promoting a sense of ownership over their behavior and learning.

Celebrate Achievements Together

- **Acknowledge Progress**: Regularly acknowledge and celebrate the progress made in addressing concerns. This recognition reinforces positive behavior and motivates continued effort.
- **Community Building**: Organize events or meetings that celebrate student achievements and foster a sense of community among families and educators.

Addressing concerns collaboratively between families and educators is vital for fostering student success. **By maintaining open communication, scheduling regular meetings, collaboratively problem-solving, establishing clear goals, monitoring progress, providing resources, and building trust, both parties can effectively support the child's development.** This partnership not only addresses immediate concerns but also strengthens the overall learning environment, ensuring that students thrive academically and socially.

"Techniques for Involving Families in Discussions about Student Behavior"

Engaging families in discussions about student behavior is vital for fostering a supportive environment that encourages positive outcomes.

Regular Communication

- **Weekly or Monthly Updates**: Send regular updates that highlight both positive behaviors and areas for improvement. This keeps families informed and provides a foundation for discussions.
- **Behavior Reports**: Create simple behavior reports that summarize students' daily or weekly behaviors, making it easy for families to understand their child's conduct at school.

Parent-Teacher Conferences

- **Focused Discussions**: Schedule regular conferences specifically to discuss behavior. Provide a safe space for families to express their concerns and share insights about their child.
- **Action Plans**: Collaborate with families during these meetings to create action plans for addressing behavioral concerns, ensuring everyone is aligned on goals and strategies.

Workshops and Training Sessions

- **Behavioral Strategies Workshops**: Offer workshops that educate families about effective behavior management techniques they can use at home, reinforcing school expectations.
- **Social-Emotional Learning Sessions**: Host sessions focused on social-emotional learning, helping families understand the importance of emotional regulation and interpersonal skills.

Positive Reinforcement Communication

- **Celebrating Positive Behavior**: Regularly share successes and positive behavior reports with families, reinforcing good behavior and encouraging continued engagement.
- **Recognition Programs**: Implement programs that recognize positive behavior, allowing families to participate in celebrating their child's achievements.

Feedback Mechanisms

- **Surveys and Questionnaires**: Use surveys to gather parent feedback on their child's behavior and their own perceptions of school practices. This helps identify areas of concern and engage families in the process.
- **Suggestion Boxes**: Provide **anonymous suggestion boxes for families to share their thoughts or concerns about behavioral expectations** and practices.

Create a Welcoming Environment

- **Open-Door Policy**: Establish an open-door policy where families feel comfortable discussing their child's behavior at any time, fostering a collaborative relationship.
- **Family Engagement Events**: Organize events that bring families into the school community, promoting dialogue and building relationships.

Utilize Technology

- **Virtual Meetings**: Offer **virtual meetings or phone calls for families who may have difficulty attending in-person discussions**, ensuring they can participate in important conversations about behavior.
- **Online Platforms**: Use school websites or apps to provide resources and information about behavior management strategies that families can implement at home.

Encourage Student Participation

- **Student-Led Discussions**: Involve students in discussions about their behavior by allowing them to share their perspectives during conferences or meetings with families.
- **Self-Reflection Activities**: Encourage students to complete self-reflection activities regarding their behavior, which can be discussed with families, promoting ownership and accountability.

Incorporate Community Resources

- **Partnerships with Local Organizations**: Collaborate with local organizations to provide additional resources for families, such as counseling or behavior management programs.
- **Community Workshops**: Host community workshops that focus on behavior management, bringing in experts to share strategies that can benefit families.

Ongoing Support and Follow-Up

- **Regular Check-Ins**: Schedule regular check-ins with families to discuss progress on behavioral goals, addressing any new concerns that may arise.
- **Summary Reports**: After meetings, provide families with summary reports that outline what was discussed and any agreed-upon action steps, keeping the conversation going.

Involving families in discussions about student behavior is essential for creating a cohesive support system that promotes positive outcomes. **By utilizing regular communication, hosting workshops, encouraging student participation, and providing ongoing support, educators can effectively engage families.** This collaboration not only addresses behavioral concerns but also strengthens the partnership between home and school, fostering a positive learning environment for all students.

"Building Partnerships for Student Success"

Building effective partnerships among educators, families, and the broader community is essential for fostering student success. **Collaborative relationships create a supportive network that enhances learning, promotes positive behavior, and addresses challenge**s.

Establish Clear Communication Channels

- **Regular Updates**: Provide consistent updates about school activities, policies, and student progress through newsletters, emails, and school websites. Keeping everyone informed fosters transparency.
- **Open-Door Policy**: Encourage open communication by welcoming families and community members to share their insights, concerns, and feedback. This helps build trust and rapport.

Involve Families in Decision-Making

- **Parent Advisory Committees**: Create committees that include family members to discuss school policies, programs, and improvements. Involving families in decision-making processes empowers them and strengthens their connection to the school.
- **Surveys and Feedback**: Regularly solicit feedback from families about school initiatives and their children's experiences. This input can guide decisions and enhance school programs.

Host Collaborative Events

- **Family Engagement Nights**: Organize events that bring families into the school community, such as family nights, workshops, or open houses. These events create opportunities for networking and relationship-building.
- **Community Partnerships**: Collaborate with local organizations to host events that benefit students and families, such as health fairs, tutoring programs, or career days.

Provide Resources and Support

- **Educational Workshops**: Offer workshops for families on topics such as academic support, behavioral management, and social-emotional learning. Empowering families with knowledge helps them support their children effectively.
- **Resource Guides**: Create resource guides that outline available community services, tutoring options, and support networks. Make this information easily accessible to families.

Encourage Student Involvement

- **Student Leadership Opportunities**: Provide opportunities for students to take on leadership roles in school activities and community projects. This fosters a sense of ownership and responsibility.
- **Service Learning Projects**: Engage students in service-learning projects that connect them with the community, promoting collaboration and social responsibility.

Foster Trust and Respect

- **Cultural Competence**: Be sensitive to the diverse backgrounds of families and the community. Understanding and respecting cultural differences fosters trust and builds stronger relationships.
- **Celebrate Diversity**: Organize events that celebrate the diverse cultures within the school community, promoting inclusivity and understanding among families and students.

Monitor and Celebrate Progress

- **Regular Check-Ins**: Establish regular check-ins with families to discuss their child's progress and any challenges. This keeps families engaged and informed.
- **Recognition Programs**: Celebrate student achievements and milestones publicly, involving families in recognizing their children's successes.

Collaborate with Community Resources

- **Partnerships with Local Organizations**: Work with local organizations, businesses, and nonprofits to provide additional resources and support for students and families, such as counseling services or mentoring programs.
- **Shared Goals**: Align school initiatives with community goals to create a unified approach to student success.

Develop a Comprehensive Support System

- **Multi-Tiered Support**: Implement a multi-tiered system of support that includes academic, behavioral, and emotional interventions, involving families in each step of the process.
- **Coordinated Services**: Coordinate services among school staff, families, and community organizations to address student needs holistically.

Evaluate and Adapt Partnerships

- **Continuous Improvement**: Regularly assess the effectiveness of partnerships and seek feedback from families and community members. Adapt strategies based on what works best for students and their families.
- **Celebrate Successes**: Share success stories that highlight the impact of partnerships on student outcomes, inspiring continued collaboration.

Building partnerships for student success requires ongoing commitment and collaboration among educators, families, and the community. **By establishing clear communication, involving families in decision-making, hosting collaborative events, and providing resources, schools can create a supportive environment that promotes positive outcomes.** Together, these partnerships not only enhance individual student success but also strengthen the entire educational community.

> ***"I truly believe that everything that we do and everyone that we meet is put in our path for a purpose. There are no accidents; we're all teachers - if we're willing to pay attention to the lessons we learn, trust our positive instincts and not be afraid to take risks or wait for some miracle to come knocking at our door."***
>
> *—Marla Gibbs*

Chapter 11

Recap of Key Strategies for Effective Classroom Management

> ***"...good teachers are priceless. They inspire you, they entertain you, and you end up learning a ton even when you don't know it."***
> *— Nicholas Sparks, "Dear John".*

Effective classroom management is essential for creating a conducive learning environment. Here's a recap of key strategies that educators can implement to foster positive behavior, enhance student engagement, and maximize instructional time:

Establish Clear Expectations

- **Define Rules and Procedures**: Clearly outline classroom rules and procedures at the beginning of the school year. Make them visible and regularly revisit them to ensure understanding.
- **Involve Students**: Engage students in the rule-making process to foster ownership and accountability.

Create a Positive Learning Environment

- **Welcoming Atmosphere**: Design a classroom that is physically inviting, with student work displayed and areas for collaboration.
- **Build Rapport**: Develop strong relationships with students through regular check-ins and by showing genuine interest in their lives.

Implement Consistent Routines

- **Daily Routines**: Establish consistent daily routines for transitions and tasks to provide structure and predictability.
- **Explicit Teaching of Procedures**: Teach and model classroom procedures explicitly, allowing time for practice and reinforcement.

Monitor and Observe Behavior

- **Proactive Monitoring**: Circulate the classroom regularly to engage with students and observe their behavior without being intrusive.
- **Use Data**: Collect data on student behavior and performance to inform management strategies and identify patterns.

Address Disruptive Behavior Promptly

- **Preventive Strategies**: Identify potential disruptions before they escalate and address them proactively.
- **Calm Responses**: Handle disruptions calmly and effectively, employing strategies like redirecting behavior or using non-verbal cues.

Promote Student Engagement

- **Interactive Learning**: Incorporate hands-on activities and technology to keep students actively involved in lessons.
- **Encourage Participation**: Create opportunities for all students to contribute and express their thoughts, particularly those who may be reluctant to engage.

Involve Families in the Process

- **Regular Communication**: Maintain open lines of communication with families about classroom expectations and student behavior.
- **Family Engagement**: Involve families in discussions about their child's behavior and academic progress, fostering a partnership for success.

Foster Student Responsibility

- **Empower Students**: Encourage self-regulation by giving students a voice in classroom decisions and management strategies.
- **Peer Mediation**: Implement peer mediation programs to help students develop conflict resolution skills.

Provide Continuous Support and Feedback

- **Regular Check-Ins**: Schedule periodic follow-ups with students to discuss their progress and any behavioral concerns.
- **Positive Reinforcement**: Recognize and celebrate positive behavior to motivate students and reinforce desired actions.

Reflect and Adapt Strategies

- **Ongoing Evaluation**: Regularly assess the effectiveness of management strategies and be open to adapting them based on student needs and feedback.
- **Professional Development**: Engage in ongoing professional development to learn new techniques and approaches for effective classroom management.

Implementing these key strategies can significantly enhance classroom management, leading to a positive and productive learning environment. **By establishing clear expectations, creating a supportive atmosphere, monitoring behavior, and fostering engagement, educators can help all students thrive academically and socially.** Effective classroom management is a dynamic process that requires reflection, adaptation, and collaboration among students, families, and educators.

"Encouragement for Teachers to Reflect on and Adapt Their Management Approaches"

Effective classroom management is not a one-size-fits-all solution; it requires ongoing reflection, adaptation, and a willingness to learn.

Embrace Growth Mindset

- **Continuous Improvement**: Remember that effective management strategies evolve. Embrace a growth mindset, viewing challenges as opportunities for learning and improvement.
- **Celebrate Progress**: Acknowledge small successes in your management approaches. Celebrating these victories can motivate you to keep refining your techniques.

Reflect Regularly

- **Self-Assessment**: Take time to reflect on your management practices. Consider what worked well, what didn't, and why. This self-assessment is crucial for growth.
- **Journaling**: Maintain a reflective journal where you can document your experiences, insights, and areas for development. This practice helps clarify your thoughts and track your progress over time.

Seek Feedback

- **Peer Collaboration**: Engage with colleagues to share experiences and strategies. Observing others and discussing their approaches can provide new insights and ideas.
- **Student Input**: Ask for feedback from students about what helps them learn best. Their perspectives can guide you in adapting your management style to better meet their needs.

Stay Informed

- **Professional Development**: Participate in workshops, courses, or webinars focused on classroom management. Staying informed about the latest research and strategies can inspire new approaches.
- **Educational Literature**: Read books and articles on effective management practices. Learning from experts in the field can provide fresh perspectives and innovative techniques.

Adapt to Student Needs

- **Individual Differences**: Recognize that each class and each student is unique. Be flexible and willing to adapt your strategies based on the specific dynamics and needs of your classroom.
- **Cultural Competence**: Consider the diverse backgrounds of your students. Tailoring your management approach to respect and incorporate their cultural perspectives can enhance engagement and cooperation.

Experiment with New Strategies

- **Trial and Error**: Don't be afraid to try new techniques or approaches. Experimentation can lead to discovering what resonates best with your students.
- **Incremental Changes**: Implement changes gradually. Small adjustments can often lead to significant improvements without overwhelming you or your students.

Focus on Relationships

- **Build Rapport**: Continuously work on building positive relationships with your students. Strong connections can enhance classroom management and create a more supportive learning environment.
- **Trust and Respect**: Foster an atmosphere of trust and respect where students feel valued and heard. This foundation makes it easier to implement and adapt management strategies.

Maintain a Positive Attitude

- **Stay Positive**: Approach classroom management challenges with positivity. Your attitude can influence the classroom climate and student behavior.
- **Resilience**: Recognize that setbacks are part of the process. Maintain resilience and focus on finding solutions rather than dwelling on difficulties.

Reflecting on and adapting your classroom management approaches is essential for fostering a successful learning environment. **By embracing a growth mindset, seeking feedback, staying informed, and focusing on relationships, you can enhance your effectiveness as an educator. Remember, the journey of improvement is ongoing—every step you take toward better management practices contributes to the overall success of your students. Your commitment to reflection and adaptation not only benefits your teaching but also positively impacts the educational experience of every student in your care.**

"My teacher gave me the best gift of all... Believing in me!"

- Unknown

"The best teacher is the one who shows you where to look but doesn't tell you what to see." — *Alexandra K. Trenfor*

www.ingramcontent.com/pod-product-compliance
Lightning Source LLC
LaVergne TN
LVHW041202150826
845673LV00001B/254

* 9 7 9 8 8 9 6 3 2 3 8 4 6 *